THE GOVERNMENT CLASS BOOK.

A Youth's Manual of Instruction in the Principles of Constitutional Government and Law.

PART I. PRINCIPLES OF GOVERNMENT;
  I. GENERAL PRINCIPLES OF GOVERNMENT.
  II. GOVERNMENT IN THE STATE.
  III. THE UNITED STATES GOVERNMENT.
PART II. PRINCIPLES OF LAW;
  I. COMMON AND STATUTORY LAW (OR MUNICIPAL LAW).
  II. INTERNATIONAL LAW.

BY ANDREW W. YOUNG,

Author of "American Statesman," "Citizen's Manual of Government and Law," etc., etc.

NEW EDITION,
THOROUGHLY REVISED
BY SALTER S. CLARK.
Counsellor at Law.

NEW YORK:
CLARK & MAYNARD, PUBLISHERS,
734 BROADWAY.
1884.

PREFACE.

There is probably none to deny that the study of the principles of political science is a necessary part of a liberal education. But in a country where the people govern themselves we believe it is more than this: it is a necessary part of a common-school education. In the United States there is the strongest reason for this, for here not only do high and low alike elect their own lawmakers and rulers, but they also establish their own constitutions and determine even the fundamental principles upon which they shall be governed. The danger of entrusting such power to the ignorant has not failed of illustration here, and lately. But having universal suffrage—for good or evil—there is but one resource, to teach the people how to govern themselves.

Nor is a knowledge of the principles of legal science less necessary to every person. The laws of man know as little of mercy as the laws of nature, in that they never admit ignorance as an excuse for wrong. It is a proof of the essential justice of our system of jurisprudence, that so many pass safely through life, totally ignorant of the law, and relying merely upon their own sense of what should be. And yet every day gives proof that ignorance is always dangerous. The study of such a work will not make a youth a lawyer, but it will fix in his mind a system of broad principles, which cannot fail to be useful practically.

Though these facts are self-evident, this study has been heretofore strangely neglected. The aim of this book, in supplying a want believed to exist, is to present, in such form as to be used chiefly as a text-book for schools, a broad and comprehensive view of the principles of government and law in the United States (which are substantially the same throughout the country), and thus to teach the young the varied rights and duties of a citizen in relation to his government and his fellow-citizens.

The book is divided into two parts.

Part I., *Principles of Government*, is devoted (after a few chapters upon general principles), first, to government by the State, and second, to government by the Nation. It is here that the book is believed to have its chief advantage over others of its kind. In all that we have examined, either one or the other of these subjects has been neglected. Many youth have grown to manhood with so little appreciation of the political importance of the State, as to believe it nothing more than a geographical division; others have placed the State too high and failed to realize the power and dignity of the Nation. In reality, the National Government, on the one hand, is of far greater historic interest and permanent political importance, as really governing the future freedom or serfdom of the race. On the other hand, the State, which says whether the particular individual shall vote, what rights of property he shall have, and what shall be the punishment for his crimes, enters far more into the daily affairs of the single citizen, touches him at more points, and is therefore of greater temporary interest. Both subjects should be studied, and it is of especial importance at this time that their relation to each other should be clearly presented to the youth of the land, for State rights and National rights have not yet finished their conflict.

Part II., *Principles of Law*, contains also two divisions, the first one presenting the main principles which govern the rights and duties of man to man in his every-day life, his varied rights connected with personal security, liberty, and property; and the second giving the rules by which the relations of nations to each other are regulated.

Thus the volume presents a general view of the position of the citizen in all the relations he may sustain in this country: to his fellow-citizen, to his State, to his Nation, and to foreign nations. Throughout the book the purpose has been to omit all details, so as not to injure the effect of the principle, even where a small untruth is implied for the sake of a larger truth.

The present revision has, it is thought, made extensive improvement, by changes and additions which the great events of the last few years have rendered necessary, by pursuing a more natural and logical order, with proper subordination of topics, by confining each paragraph of the chapter to a single subject and supplying it with a title, and by the addition of schemes, where appropriate, to be used as blackboard exercises, and of review questions for the use of both pupil and teacher. It is confidently hoped that the book in this revision may find as much favor as has been kindly shown it in the past.

S S. C.

New York, June 21, 1880.

ANALYSIS OF CONTENTS.

- **PART I.—PRINCIPLES OF GOVERNMENT;**
  - **Div. I.—General Principles;**
  - **Div. II.—State Governments;**
    - Sec. I.—Introductory,
    - Sec. II.—Legislative Department,
    - Sec. III.—Executive Department,
    - Sec. IV.—Judicial Department.
  - **Div. III.—The National Government;**
    - Sec. I.—Its Origin and Nature,
    - Sec. II.—Legislative Department,
    - Sec. III.—Executive Department,
    - Sec. IV.—Judicial Department,
    - Sec. V.—Miscellaneous Provisions.
- **PART II.—PRINCIPLES OF LAW;**
  - **Div. I.—Municipal Law;**
    - Sec. I.—Civil Rights in General,
    - Sec. II.—Contracts,
    - Sec. III.—Real Estate,
    - Sec. IV.—Criminal Law.
  - **Div. II.—International Law;**
    - Sec. I.—Peaceful Relations of Nations,
    - Sec. II.—Relations of Nations in War.

CONTENTS.

PART I.

PRINCIPLES OF GOVERNMENT.

DIVISION I.

GENERAL PRINCIPLES.

	PAGE
Chapter I. Mankind fitted for Society, Government, and Law.	11
Chapter II. Rights, Liberty, and Law, classified	13
Chapter III. Different Forms of Government	19

DIVISION II.

STATE GOVERNMENTS.

SECTION I.—INTRODUCTORY.

THEIR BASIS—THE CONSTITUTION: ELECTIONS: THREE DEPARTMENTS.

Chapter IV. Constitutions: Their Nature, Object, and Establishment	23
Chapter V. Qualifications of Electors	26
Chapter VI. Elections	28
Chapter VII. Division of Powers of Government	31

SECTION II.

LEGISLATIVE DEPARTMENT.

Chapter VIII. Legislature: how constituted	34
Chapter IX. Meetings and Organization	37
Chapter X. Manner of Enacting Laws	40

SECTION III.

EXECUTIVE DEPARTMENT.

		PAGE
Chapter	XI. State Officers...................................	45
Chapter	XII. County Officers...............................	49
Chapter	XIII. Town Officers................................	54
Chapter	XIV. Cities and Villages........................	56
Chapter	XV. Taxes...	60
Chapter	XVI. Education.....................................	65
Chapter	XVII. Public Institutions........................	69
Chapter	XVIII. Militia..	72

SECTION IV.

JUDICIAL DEPARTMENT.

Chapter	XIX. Courts...	75
Chapter	XX. Legal Proceedings........................	79

DIVISION III.

THE NATIONAL GOVERNMENT.

SECTION I.

ITS ORIGIN AND NATURE.

Chapter	XXI. Government before the Revolution.........	90
Chapter	XXII. The Confederation........................	93
Chapter	XXIII. The Union under the Constitution.........	97
Chapter	XXIV. Constitution of the United States..........	100

SECTION II.

LEGISLATIVE DEPARTMENT.

Chapter	XXV. House of Representatives.................	124
Chapter	XXVI. Senate.......................................	128
Chapter	XXVII. General Legislative Regulations............	131
Chapter	XXVIII. Powers of Taxation......................	133
Chapter	XXIX. Power to Regulate Commerce.............	136
Chapter	XXX. Other Powers relating to Peace...........	140
Chapter	XXXI. Powers relating to War...................	147
Chapter	XXXII. Prohibitions on the United States.........	152
Chapter	XXXIII. Prohibitions on the States................	155

SECTION III.
EXECUTIVE DEPARTMENT.

		PAGE
Chapter	XXXIV. President and Vice-President : Election, Qualifications, etc.	160
Chapter	XXXV. Powers and Duties of the President	163
Chapter	XXXVI. Auxiliary Executive Departments	168

SECTION IV.
JUDICIAL DEPARTMENT.

Chapter XXXVII. National Courts and their Jurisdiction	171
Chapter XXXVIII. Treason	176

SECTION V.
MISCELLANEOUS PROVISIONS.

Chapter	XXXIX. Relations of States	178
Chapter	XL. Amendment: Debt: Supremacy: Oath: Test: Ratification	181
Chapter	XLI. The First Twelve Amendments	183
Chapter	XLII. The 13th, 14th, and 15th Amendments	189

PART II.
PRINCIPLES OF LAW.

DIVISION I.
MUNICIPAL LAW.

SECTION I.
CIVIL RIGHTS IN GENERAL.

Chapter	XLIII. Absolute Civil Rights	195
Chapter	XLIV. Relative Civil Rights	199

SECTION II.
CONTRACTS.

Chapter	XLV. Contracts in General	202
Chapter	XLVI. Marriage	208

		PAGE
Chapter XLVII.	Principal and Agent	211
Chapter XLVIII.	Partnership	214
Chapter XLIX.	Sales of Personal Property	217
Chapter L	Gifts: Fraudulent Transfers	220
Chapter LI.	Promissory Notes and Bills of Exchange	221
Chapter LII.	Services	228
Chapter LIII.	Insurance	230
Chapter LIV.	Shipping	232
Chapter LV.	Interest	234

SECTION III.
REAL ESTATE.

Chapter LVI.	Estates in Real Property	235
Chapter LVII.	Deeds and Mortgages	237
Chapter LVIII.	Appurtenances	239
Chapter LIX.	Landlord and Tenant	242
Chapter LX.	Distribution of Property upon Death	245

SECTION IV.
CRIMINAL LAW.

Chapter LXI.	Crimes	249

DIVISION II.
INTERNATIONAL LAW.

SECTION I.
PEACEFUL RELATIONS OF NATIONS.

Chapter LXII.	Nature and Authority of International Law	256
Chapter LXIII.	Ordinary Rules of Peace	260

SECTION II.
RELATIONS OF NATIONS IN WAR.

Chapter LXIV.	Causes and Objects of War	264
Chapter LXV.	Rights and Duties of Belligerents	266
Chapter LXVI.	Rights and Duties of Neutrals	270

PRINCIPLES
OF
GOVERNMENT AND LAW.

PART I.
PRINCIPLES OF GOVERNMENT.

DIVISION I.
GENERAL PRINCIPLES.

CHAPTER I.

MANKIND FITTED FOR SOCIETY, GOVERNMENT, AND LAW.

1. Mankind Social. — Men are by nature fitted for society. By this we mean that they are naturally disposed to associate with each other. They could not be happy without such association. Hence we conclude that the Creator has designed men for society.

2. Dependent on Each Other.—Man is so formed that he is dependent upon his fellow-men. He has not the natural strength of other animals. We can hardly imagine how a person could defend himself against the beasts, or even procure the necessaries of life, without assistance from his fellow-beings. But by means of conversation they are enabled to improve their reason and increase their knowledge, and to find methods of supplying their wants, and of improving their social condition.

3. Each Must Support Himself.—But, although men need the assistance of each other, society is so formed that each must have the care of himself. If every man were fed and clothed from a common store, provided by the labor of all, many, depending upon the labor of others, would be less industrious than they now are. By the present arrangement, which obliges every man to provide for his own wants, more is produced, a greater number are cared for, and the general welfare is better promoted than would be done if each labored for the benefit of all.

4. Right of Property.—From this arrangement comes the right of property. If each man's earnings should go into a common stock for the use of all, there would be nothing that any one could call his own. But if each is to provide for himself, he must have a right to use and enjoy the fruits of his own labor.

5. Common to All.—But all men in society have the same rights. Therefore we cannot rightfully supply our own wants or gratify our own desires any further than is consistent with the rights of others. But man is by nature selfish, and many would infringe the rights of others, for their own selfish ends, unless restrained. Hence we see the necessity of some fixed rules that each one may know what he may do, and what he must not do.

6. Law.—These rules for regulating the social actions of men are called laws. *Law*, in a general sense, is a rule of action, and is applied to all kinds of action; as, the law of gravitation, the laws of chemistry, etc. But in a limited sense, it denotes the rules of human action prescribing what men are to do, and forbidding what they are not to do.

7. Man a Moral Being.—We have seen that man is fitted for law, because he is designed for society, and law is necessary to govern society. But by nature, also, he is fitted for government and law, because he is a *moral* being. The word *moral* has various significations. When we say, a moral man, we mean a virtuous or upright man. But in a wider sense it relates to the social actions of men, both right and wrong, as when we say, his morals are good, or his morals are bad. When it is said that man is a moral being, it is meant that he has a sense of right and wrong, or at least the power of acquiring it. He knows what is right and what is wrong, and he knows that he ought to do the right and avoid the wrong. Therefore he is fitted to understand why laws are right.

    8. **Government Necessary.**—Thus we have seen that men are social, reasonable, and moral beings, and that for each one of those reasons they are fitted for society and law. But law cannot exist without government. Law is a rule of action laid down by the supreme power, and if there is no supreme power there can be no law. Hence we see the necessity for government. It is not probable that people knowingly acted on these principles in first forming governments; that is, deliberately met together and agreed to have a certain government and certain laws. But it is those principles that maintain them now.

CHAPTER II.

RIGHTS, LIBERTY, AND LAW, CLASSIFIED.

    1. **Rights.**—A right is a just claim. We have a right to what we have acquired by honest labor, or other lawful means, because we are justly entitled to freely use and enjoy it. We have a right to our lives, and to our freedom, that is to do whatever we think necessary for our own safety and happiness, provided we do not trespass upon the

rights of others, because it would be unjust to deprive us of our lives or freedom.

2. How Forfeited. — But society has its rights also, and if we infringe them it is just we should be punished by losing some of our own. We may forfeit them by some offence or crime. If, for example, a man is fined for breaking a law, he loses his right to the money he is obliged to pay. By stealing, he forfeits his liberty, and may be justly imprisoned. By committing murder, he forfeits his right to life, and may be hanged.

3. Political Rights. — Rights are *political* or *civil*. *Political rights* are those which each citizen has with reference to sharing in the government. The word *political*, in a general sense, relates to the government. The whole body of the people united under one government is called the political body, or body politic. The right of the people to choose and establish for themselves a form of government, or constitution, and the right to elect persons to make and execute the laws, are political rights. The right of voting at elections is therefore a political right. Political rights are derived from the constitution. Under absolute monarchies, therefore, where there is no constitution, the people have no political rights; under democracies they have more than under any other form of government.

4. Civil Rights are all those which are not *political*. They are the rights which govern our ordinary, every-day actions; such as, the right to go where we please, to do whatever we wish with our own property, or to control our children. They are also called *natural rights*, because given to us by nature, or by birth; and sometimes *inalienable rights*, because they cannot justly be taken away from us. They are called *civil* because they relate to the ordinary duties of a citizen.

5. Absolute Civil Rights.—Civil rights are either *absolute* or *relative*. The *absolute civil* rights are such as we have as individuals, as members of society, in our relations to all the other members of society. They are divided into three classes: the right of *personal security*, which is the right to be secure from injury to our lives, body, health, or reputation; the right of *personal liberty*, which is the right to go wherever we please; and the right of *private property*, or the right to acquire property and enjoy it without disturbance. These are often called *personal rights*, or the *rights of persons*. The term *rights of person* includes only the first two; viz., the rights of *personal security* and *personal liberty*. *Religious rights*, which consist in the right to worship God in whatever way each one thinks best, and to make known and maintain his religious beliefs, are absolute rights.

6. Relative Civil Rights are such as we have in our relations to particular persons or classes. They are either *public* or *private*. The *public relative civil rights* are those we have in our relations to the government (except the right to share in it); as, the right to be protected by it, and the right the government and its officers have to our obedience. The *private relative civil rights* are such as are connected with the four relations of husband and wife, parent and child, guardian and ward, and employer and employed; as, the right of the parent to the obedience of the child, or the right of the wife to be supported by her husband.

7. Liberty is the being free to exercise and enjoy our rights, and is called natural, political, civil, or religious, according to the particular class of rights referred to. Thus the exercise of rights guaranteed by the constitution or political law is called political liberty. The free enjoyment of rights secured by the civil or municipal laws is called civil liberty. And freedom of religious opinion and worship is called religious liberty. *Freedom of speech* and *freedom of the press* mean the liberty to speak and print whatever we choose, provided we do not abuse the right.

8. Law.—But it is easy to see that it makes little difference how many rights a man has, unless there is some power to ensure him the liberty to enjoy them. The object of law is to secure to all men the various kinds of rights we have described. It has different names, corresponding to the kinds of rights which it protects; as, the *political law*, which secures our *political rights*, and the *civil* or *municipal law*, which secures our *civil rights*. The word *municipal* was used by the Romans to designate that which related to a *municipium;* i.e., a free town, or city. And so, often, we use the term *municipal law* as denoting the law that relates to cities or towns, but here it is used in a broader sense, and includes the body of laws which prescribe what we may, or must not, do, and is equivalent to *civil law.** The constitution is the *political law;* the body of laws governing the ordinary actions of men is the *civil* or *municipal law;* and the rules which regulate the intercourse of nations with each other constitute *international law*.

9. The Moral Law is that which prescribes man's duties not only to his fellow-men, but also to God. It is briefly expressed in the decalogue, or ten commandments, and is still more briefly summed up in the two great commandments, to love God with all our heart, and to love our neighbor as ourselves. It is sometimes called the *divine law*, because God is its author, and the *revealed law*, or *law*

---

* Care must be taken to distinguish the term, as used in this connection, from the Civil Law, a name for the old Roman law.

of revelation, because it is revealed to man in the Scriptures. As a rule of conduct it is also the same as the *law of nature*, the only difference between them being in their origin; the former, the *revealed law*, coming directly from God, and the latter, the *law of nature*, coming from nature—that is, our own consciousness in its perfect state.

10. Broader than Civil Law.—Although the moral law is a perfect rule of action, to which all human laws ought to conform, yet the civil law does not, and cannot, embrace all that the moral law does. The moral law is directed not only to the outward acts, but also to the thoughts and intents of the heart. It requires us to love our Creator supremely, and our neighbor as ourselves; in other words, to do to others as we would that they should do to us. But as the omniscient God only knows when men fail in these duties, no human authority could enforce such a law. Human laws, therefore, have respect chiefly to the outward acts of men, and are designed to regulate their intercourse with each other.

Rights of Citizens.

I. **POLITICAL**; these are
  1. Right of all to establish a government, and
  2. Right of each to share in it, by voting.

II. **CIVIL**; these are
  1. **ABSOLUTE**; they are the right of
     1. Personal Security,
     2. Personal Liberty, and
     3. Private Property.
  2. **RELATIVE**; these are
     1. **Public**; they are
        1. Right of people to protection of government, and
        2. Right of government to obedience of people.
     2. **Private**; arising from relations of
        1. Husband and wife,
        2. Parent and child,
        3. Guardian and ward, and
        4. Employer and employed.

CHAPTER III.

DIFFERENT FORMS OF GOVERNMENT.

1. Patriarchal Government.—Governments have existed in a great variety of forms. Most existing governments are, more or less, mixtures of the different kinds. The earliest governments of which we have any knowledge are the patriarchal. *Patriarch*, from the Greek *pater*, father, and *archos*, chief, or head, means the father and ruler of a family. This kind of government prevailed in the early ages of the world, and is the form adapted to a state of society where the people dwell together in families or tribes, and are not yet formed into states or nations. Abraham was a patriarchal ruler.

2. Theocracy.—After their departure from Egypt, the government of the Hebrews was a *theocracy*. This word is from *theos*, God, and *kratos*, power, and signifies a government by those who are also the religious rulers, or, as it is claimed, by the immediate direction of God. The laws by which they were governed they believed were given to them on Mount Sinai by God himself, their leader and king.

3. Most Common Forms.—But the most common forms of government are monarchy, aristocracy, and democracy. Many claim that all kinds of government may be reduced to one of these three. For example, the patriarchal government is but a kind of monarchy. The power of government is, in a general sense, called the *supreme* power, or *sovereignty*.

4. Monarchy.—The form of government in which the

supreme power is in the hands of one person is called a *monarchy*. The word *monarch* is from two Greek words, *monos*, sole or only, and *archos*, a chief; and is a general name for a single ruler, whether he is called king, emperor, or prince. A government in which all power resides in or proceeds from one person is an *absolute* monarchy. If the power of the monarch is restrained by laws or by some other power, it is called a *limited* monarchy. The English Government is a limited monarchy. A monarchy is called *hereditary* in which the throne passes from father to son, or from the monarch to his successor, by inheritance. On the death of a sovereign, the eldest son is usually heir to the crown. A monarchy is *elective* where, on the death of the ruler, his successor is appointed by an election. Only a few such monarchies have existed.

5. **Despotism.**—An absolute monarchy is sometimes called *despotism*. The words *despot* and *tyrant* at first meant simply a *single* ruler. They are now applied, for the most part, to rulers who exercise authority over their subjects with severity. In an absolute despotism, the monarch has entire control over his subjects. They have no law but the will of the ruler, who has at command a large force of armed men to keep his people in subjection. The governments of Russia and Turkey are more despotic than any others in Europe.

6. **Aristocracy** is the form of government in which the power is exercised by a privileged order of men, distinguished for their rank and wealth. The word *aristocracy* is from the Greek word *aristos*, best, and *kratos*, power, or *krateo*, to govern; and meant, originally, government by the best men. It is also used for the nobility of a country under a monarchical government. *Nobles* are persons of rank above the common people, and bear some title of honor. The titles of the English nobility are duke, marquis,

earl, viscount, and baron. These titles are hereditary, being derived from birth. In some cases they are conferred upon persons by the king.

7. Democracy is government by the people; the word democracy being from the Greek *demos*, the people, and *krateo*, to govern. In a government purely democratic, the great body of freemen meet in one assembly to make and execute the laws. There were some such governments in ancient Greece; but they necessarily comprised small territories, scarcely more than a single town. The freemen of a state could not all meet in a single assembly.

8. A Republic is that kind of democracy in which the power to enact and execute the laws is exercised by representatives, who are persons elected by the people to act for them. The people not only enact the laws and execute them through the representatives whom they elect, but also adopt their own constitution or form of government, and thus all power comes from the people, the government being properly called a *representative democracy*. A republic is sometimes also called a *commonwealth*, because its object is the common happiness of all.

9. In this Country the people are everywhere under two governments, the State and the National Government. The United States is a republic, and so, also, is each State. Each State has given up to the Nation those powers and duties which naturally belong to a nation in its relations with foreign powers, as the right to make war or treaties, and also has given up the power to make laws on subjects in which all the people in the country are interested together, as commerce, the coining of money, and patents. But the State retains all the powers it has not given up, and both State and National Governments are independent of each other, each in its own sphere. The *Territories*, until they become States, are under the United States

Government. It grants them, to a certain extent, through Congress, self-government, on the plan of the State governments, but it can take it away at any time.

Kinds of Government.

I. **MONARCHY**; this may be,
- 1. **As to Power**,
  - 1. Absolute, or
  - 2. Limited.
- 2. **As to Title**,
  - 1. Hereditary, or
  - 2. Elective.

II. **ARISTOCRACY**;

III. **DEMOCRACY**; this may be,
- 1. **Pure Democracy**, or
- 2. **Republic**.

DIVISION II.

State Governments.

SECTION I.—INTRODUCTORY.

Their Basis, the Constitution; Elections; Three Departments.

CHAPTER IV.

CONSTITUTIONS: THEIR NATURE, OBJECT, AND ESTABLISHMENT.

1. Republic the Best Government.—Of all the different forms of government which have existed, a republican government, on the plan of that which has been established in this country, is believed to be best adapted to secure the liberties of a people, and to promote the general welfare. Under the reign of a wise and virtuous ruler, the rights of person and property may be fully enjoyed, and the people may be in a good degree prosperous. But the requisite virtue and wisdom combined have seldom been found in any one man (i.e., a monarchy), or a body of men (i.e., an aristocracy). And, as we in this country believe, experience has proved that the objects of civil government may be best secured by a written constitution founded upon the will or consent of the people. Each State in the Union has such a constitution, and the Nation itself has one.

2. Constitution.—The word *constitute* is from the Latin, and signifies *to set*, to fix, to establish. *Constitution*, when used in a political sense, means the established form of government of a state. In a free government, like ours, it is properly called the *political law*, being established by the people as a body politic. (Page 14, § 3.) It is also called the *fundamental law*, because it is the *foundation* of all other laws of the state, and of all the powers of the state, legislative, executive, and judicial.

3. **Nature.**—A constitution is in the nature of an agreement between a whole community, or body politic, and each of its members. This agreement or contract implies that each one binds himself to the whole, and the whole bind themselves to each one, that all shall be governed by certain laws and regulations for the common good.

4. **Convention.**—In forming a constitution, the people must act collectively. But their number is too large to meet in a single assembly. Therefore they choose a small number to act for them. One or more are chosen in each county, or smaller district, and are called delegates. A *delegate* is a person appointed by another with power to transact business as his representative. The assembly composed of the delegates so elected is called a *convention:* a name given to most public meetings other than legislative assemblies. The convention draws up in proper form a paper containing the fundamental laws and general form of government, under which it thinks the people wish to be governed.

5. **Adoption by People.**—But what has thus been prepared by the convention is not yet a constitution. It is only a draft of one, and cannot, in general, become a constitution without the consent of the people to be given at an election. If a majority of the persons voting at such election vote in favor of the proposed constitution, it is adopted, and becomes the constitution of the State.

6. Amendment.—A constitution usually provides for its own amendment. Amendments are, generally, proposed and passed by the legislature, sometimes on two successive years, and then submitted to the people.

7. Value.—One of the most valuable rights of the people under a free government is the right to have a constitution of their own choice. Indeed it is in this right that their freedom principally consists. It is by the constitution that their rights are secured. The legislature can pass no laws that the constitution forbids, and if they should enact unjust and oppressive laws, the people, having by their constitution reserved the right to displace them, may do so by electing others in their stead.*

8. Other Governments.—In an absolute monarchy the people have neither the right to establish their own form of government, nor the right to elect their law-makers. The will of the monarch is the only law. In a limited monarchy they have some political rights. In Great Britain the people elect representatives to the House of Commons, which is the most important part of the legislature; but they did not originally establish the form of government. The English have no written constitution. What is called the English constitution consists of the body of fundamental laws, principles, and customs which in the course of centuries have become securely fixed. But Parliament, the English law-making body, has the power to make any law it sees fit.

---

*It would seem to follow from this that the people of any State, having the right to select their own form of government, might, if they wished, choose any form; for example, a monarchy. But it must be remembered that this country is a nation, and not a collection of States, and that every state constitution is subject to the United States Constitution, which has guaranteed to every State in the Union a republican government, or, in other words, forbidden them to establish any other form.

CHAPTER V.

QUALIFICATIONS OF ELECTORS.

1. Electors.—One of the first provisions usually inserted in the constitution of a free state is that which declares who shall be allowed to take a part in the government; that is, to whom the political power shall be intrusted. The political power of the people consists chiefly in the right to vote, called the *right of suffrage*. The constitution regulates this, and does not give it to every one in the state, but only to such as are qualified to exercise it understandingly. Those who have the right of suffrage are called *electors*.* When, therefore, we speak of the people politically, we mean those only who are qualified electors.

2. Age.—An elector must be twenty-one years of age. Before that age young men have not the necessary knowledge and judgment to act with discretion. Some are competent at an earlier age; but a constitution can make no distinction between citizens. It has, therefore, in accordance with the general opinion, fixed the time at the age of twenty-one when men shall be deemed capable of exercising the rights and performing the duties of freemen.

3. Sex.—It is a general rule that no female can vote. The question is now being agitated in some quarters whether they should not be allowed to.

4. Residence.—That a man may vote understandingly, he must have resided long enough in the State to have become acquainted with its government and laws, and to

---

* These are not Presidential Electors. The word is used here in a general sense. For Presidential Electors, see page 161.

have learned the character and qualifications of the persons for whom he votes. State constitutions therefore require that electors shall have resided in the State for a specified period of time, varying, however, in the different States from three months to two years. In most of the States they must also have resided for some months in the county or district, and be residents of the town in which they offer to vote.

5. **Aliens.**—Persons born in foreign countries are *aliens*, and have no right to vote, though residing here. They are presumed to have too little knowledge of our government, and to feel too little interest in public affairs, on their first coming hither, to be duly qualified for the exercise of political power. Laws, however, have been enacted for naturalizing aliens after they shall have resided here long enough to become acquainted with and attached to our government. By naturalization they become citizens, entitled to all the privileges of native or natural-born citizens. (See page 141.)

6. **Criminals.**—It is provided also in state constitutions that electors convicted of infamous crimes are disfranchised. *Franchise* is a right or privilege. The right of voting is called the *elective franchise;* and an elector when deprived of this privilege is *disfranchised.* Men guilty of high crimes are deemed unfit to be intrusted with so important a duty as that of electing the persons who are to make and execute the laws of the State. It is provided, however, that if such persons are pardoned before the expiration of the term for which they were sentenced to be imprisoned, their forfeited rights are restored.

7. **Idiots** and *lunatics* have no right to vote, for the reason that they cannot use it understandingly.

8. **Property.**—In general it is not now necessary for an elector to own property. By the earliest constitutions of

many of the old States, electors were required to own property, or to have paid rents or taxes, to a certain amount. In the constitutions of the newer States, and the amended constitutions of the old States, property has not been made a qualification of an elector. *Paupers,* however, have no vote.

9. Color.—There is now no distinction of color in the right to vote, and the negro has the same privilege as the white man in all the States. Up to the adoption of the fifteenth amendment to the Constitution of the United States, in 1870, colored people, whether slave or free, could not vote in the Southern States, and in only three or four of the Northern States.

Thus it will be seen that while all the people in a State have civil rights, less than half have political rights.

CHAPTER VI.

ELECTIONS.

1. When Held.—For the convenient exercise of political power, as well as for the purposes of government generally, the territory of a State is divided into districts of small extent. A State is divided into counties, and these are divided into towns or townships. The people of every county and every town have power to manage their local concerns. The electors of the State meet every year in their respective towns for the election of officers. Governors in most of the States are elected every two or four years, but many officers elected by the people are chosen every year. All the electors of the State may vote for state officers, but only residents of the respective towns or counties can vote for the town and county officers. In most States the general state election is held in October or November.

2. **Inspectors of Election.**—Elections are conducted by persons designated by law, or chosen by the electors of the town, for that purpose. It is their duty to preserve order, and to see that the business is properly done. They are usually called *judges of election* or *inspectors of election*. Persons also (usually two) serve as clerks. Each clerk keeps a list of the names of the persons voting, which is called a *poll-list*. *Poll*, which is said to be a Saxon word, signifies *head*, and has come to mean person. By a further change it has been made to signify an election or the place where the voting is done.

3. **Voting.**—The polls, i.e. the voting places, are generally open one day, from sunrise to sunset. The inspectors receive from each voter a ballot, which is a piece of paper containing the names of the persons voted for, and the title of the office to which each of them is to be elected. The voting in most of the States is by ballot, but in one or two it is *viva voce;* that is, by the elector speaking the name of the person for whom he votes.

4. **Challenging.**—If no objection is made to an elector's voting, the ballot is put into the box and the clerks enter his name on the poll-list. If the inspectors suspect that a person offering to vote is not a qualified elector, they may question him upon his oath in respect to his age, the term of his residence in the State and county, and citizenship. Any bystander also may question his right to vote. This is called *challenging*. A person thus challenged is not allowed to vote until the challenge is withdrawn, or his qualifications are either proved by the testimony of other persons or sworn to by himself.

5. Registration.—In a few States the voters are registered, especially in the large cities. A list is made some days before the election of the names of all who present themselves and, upon examination, are shown to be qualified electors; and those only whose names have been registered are allowed to vote on election-day. Thus many interruptions to voting by the examination of voters at the polls, and much illegal voting, are prevented.

6. Canvassing.—After the polls are closed, the box is opened and the ballots are counted. This is called *canvassing* the votes. If the number of ballots agrees with the number of names on the poll-lists, it is presumed no mistake has been made either in voting or in keeping the lists. If there are more ballots than names, in some States the election will be void, in others a number of ballots equivalent to the excess will be drawn out and destroyed. If the election is one for the choosing of town officers, it is there determined who are elected, and their election is publicly declared. The election of county and state officers cannot be determined by the town canvassers. A statement of the votes given in each town for the persons voted for is sent to the county canvassers, who, from the returns of votes from all the towns, determine and declare the election of the officers chosen for the county. To determine the election of state officers, and of such others as are elected for districts comprising more than one county, a statement of the votes given for the several candidates is sent by the several boards of county canvassers to the state canvassers, who, from the returns of votes from the several counties, determine the election of the state officers.

7. Number Necessary.—In most of the States persons are elected by a plurality of votes. An election by *plurality* is when the person elected has received a higher num-

Introductory. 31

ber of votes than any other, though such number be less than half of all the votes given. Suppose, for example, three candidates receive 1000 votes: One receives 450; another, 300; the third, 250 votes. The first, having the highest number, though not a majority, is elected. In most of the States of New England a *majority*—that is, more than one half of all the votes given—is necessary to the election of many of the higher officers. The least number of votes out of 1000 by which a person can be elected by this rule is 501.

8. Objections.—Either of these modes is open to objection. When a simple plurality effects an election, 1000 votes may be so divided upon three candidates as to elect one by 334 votes; or of four candidates, one may be elected by 251 votes, and against the wishes of nearly three fourths of the electors. The objection to the other mode is that if no person receives a majority of all the votes, another election must be held. Numerous trials have, in some instances, been necessary to effect a choice; and the people of a district have remained for a time without a representative in the state or national legislature.

CHAPTER VII.

DIVISION OF POWERS OF GOVERNMENT.

1. Three Departments.—Government is divided into three distinct divisions, or, in other words, sovereign power may be exercised in three directions: in making laws, in enforcing them, and in judging whether particular cases come under certain laws. In all free countries these powers are exercised by three separate departments, called the *legislative, executive,* and *judicial* departments. In a monarchy, though they may exist, the other two are more or less under the control of the executive department, the monarch. In this country the three departments exist in every State and are kept distinct from each other.

2. Legislative.—The legislative department is that by which the laws of the State are made, and is called the *legislature.* Its object is to make such laws as the constitution does not provide for. The constitution establishes not only the form and the departments of government, but also certain broad principles of law, which the legislature cannot violate; but it leaves to the legislature the making of the particular laws to carry out those principles in detail, and there are many subjects on which the legislature is unrestrained. It would be impossible for a State to adopt, as a constitution, a system of laws that would not need change and addition.

3. Its Divisions.—The legislature is composed of two bodies, or houses, as they are called, the members of each being elected by the people. Both must agree to a measure before it becomes a law. In limited monarchies where one branch of the legislature is elective, the other is an aristocratic body, composed of men of wealth and dignity, as the British House of Lords.

4. Executive.—The executive department is intrusted with the power of executing, or carrying into effect, the laws of the State. Its principal officer is a governor, who is elected by the people. He is assisted by a number of other officers, some of whom are elected by the people; others are appointed in such manner as the constitution or laws prescribe.

5. Judicial.—The judicial department is that by which

justice is administered to the citizens. Its duty is to decide the meaning of laws, and whether particular cases fall within them. It embraces the several courts of the State. All judges and justices of the peace are judicial officers.

6. Separation.—Experience has shown the propriety of dividing the civil power into these three departments, and of confining the officers of each department to the powers and duties belonging to the same. Those who make the laws should not exercise the power of executing them; nor should they who either make or execute the laws sit in judgment over those who are brought before them for trial. It would give too much power to one, and would endanger the liberty of the people. Yet in many instances this principle is violated to a degree. In many States the governor must approve a measure before it can become a law, and thus he has legislative power. In some he appoints the judges, and so has judicial power. In some the legislature in certain cases elects the governor, and thus has some control over the executive department.

DEPARTMENTS OF GOVERNMENT.

I. **LEGISLATIVE—LAW-MAKING:** consists of
- 1. Senate,
- 2. House of Representatives, and
- 3. Governor (in many States).

II. **EXECUTIVE—LAW-EXECUTING:** represented by
- 1. Governor, and
- 2. All other executive officers.

III. **JUDICIAL—LAW-INTERPRETING AND APPLYING:** consists of
All the judges.

SECTION II.

LEGISLATIVE DEPARTMENT.

CHAPTER VIII.

LEGISLATURE: HOW CONSTITUTED.

1. Two Houses.—The legislature of every State in the Union is composed of two houses—a *senate* and a *house of representatives*, sometimes called the *upper* and *lower house*.* In most of the States the two houses together are called the *general assembly*.

a. Senate.

2. Character.—The senate, as well as the other house, is a representative body, its members being elected by the people to represent them. It is a much smaller body than

---

* Though both are representative bodies, only the lower house is called the "House of Representatives." The reason for this may be: Under the governments of the Colonies, while yet subject to Great Britain, there was but one representative assembly. The other branch of the legislature was called a *council*, consisting of a small number of men who were appointed by the King. After the Colonies became free and independent States the *senate* was substituted for the old *council*, and the other house kept its old name.

The lower house in the States of New York, Wisconsin, Nevada, and California is called the assembly; in Maryland, Virginia, and West Virginia, the house of delegates; in North Carolina, the house of commons; and in New Jersey, the general assembly.

the lower house, and consists, generally, of from twenty-five to fifty members in the different States. It was designed to be, and is, a more select body, composed of men chosen with reference to their superior ability or their greater experience in public affairs.

3. Terms.—Senators are chosen for terms of four years in about half the States; in the rest for terms of one, two, or three years. In most of the States in which senators are elected for longer terms than one year, they are not all elected at the same time. They are divided into classes, and those of one class go out of office one year, and those of another class another year; so that only a part of the senators are elected every year, or every two, or three, or four years.

4. Apportionment.—This means the division of the State into portions; from each portion its inhabitants elect one senator. Senators are differently apportioned in different States. In some States they are apportioned among the several counties, so that the number to be elected in each county shall be in proportion to the number of its inhabitants. In others they are elected by districts, equal in number to the number of senators to be chosen in the State, and a senator is elected in each district. The districts are to contain, as nearly as may be, an equal number of inhabitants, and sometimes they comprise several counties.

b. House of Representatives.

5. Character.—This house also is elective, and is a larger body than the senate. It consists, generally, of from one hundred to two hundred members in the different States.

6. Terms.—In most of the States they are elected for two years' terms; in the others, chiefly the Eastern States, annually.

7. Apportionment.—Since the number of representatives is much larger than that of senators, the districts from which they are elected will, in the same State, be much smaller. Representatives are apportioned among the counties in proportion to the population in each. In some States they are elected in districts of equal population, counties being sometimes divided in the formation of districts. In the New England States representatives are apportioned among the towns.

c. Provisions affecting both.

8. Census.—The different modes of apportioning members of the legislature have in view the same object—equal representation; that is, giving a member to the same number of inhabitants throughout the State. But in some counties the population increases more rapidly than in others. The representation then becomes unequal, being no longer in proportion to population. In order to keep the representation throughout the State as nearly equal as possible, the constitution requires that, at stated times, the people of the State shall be numbered, and a new apportionment of senators and representatives be made among the several counties according to the number of inhabitants in each county; or if the State is one in which members of the legislature are chosen in districts, a new division of the State is made into districts. This enumeration or numbering of the people is called the *census,* and is taken in some States every ten years, in others oftener. But many States depend on the census which the United States takes every ten years.

9. Qualifications.—The constitution also prescribes the qualifications of senators and representatives. If, as qualifications for an elector, full age, citizenship, and a considerable term of residence in the State and county are properly required, as we have seen (page 26), they must be at least equally necessary for those who make the laws. In no State, therefore, are any but qualified electors eligible to the office of senator or representative. In some States greater age and longer residence are required; and in some the age and term of residence have been still further increased in the case of senators. The property qualification formerly necessary for members of the legislature, as well as for voters, has been almost entirely abolished.

10. Vacancy.—If a member of the legislature dies or resigns his office before the expiration of the term for which he was chosen, the vacancy is filled by the election of another person at the next general election, or at a special election called for that purpose, or in such other manner as the constitution may provide. But a person chosen to fill a vacancy holds the office only for the remainder of the term of him whose place he was chosen to supply.

11 **Salary.**—Each member has a salary, fixed by law.

CHAPTER IX.

MEETINGS AND ORGANIZATION.

1. How Often.—The legislature meets as often as the constitution requires: in about half of the States annually, in the others biennially, or once in two years. A legislative session includes the daily meetings of a legislature from the time of its first assembling to the day of final adjournment. Thus we say the session commenced in January and ended in March. The word *session* has reference also to a single sitting, from the hour at which the members assemble on any day to the time of adjournment on the same day. Thus we say the legislature holds a daily session of four hours; or, it holds two sessions a day, as the case may be.

2. **Place.**—Meetings of the legislature are held at a certain place permanently fixed by law of the State, at which the principal state officers keep their offices. Hence it is called the *seat of government*, or, perhaps more frequently, the *capital* of the State. *Capital* is from the Latin *caput*, the head, and has come to mean chief, or the highest. In this country the word *capital*, applied to a city, now generally indicates the seat of government.

3. **Organization.**—When the two houses have assembled in their respective chambers, and the oath of office has been administered, each house proceeds to *organize*. This consists in appointing proper officers, and in determining the right of members to their seats. Each house is the sole judge of who has been elected to it. The first officer elected is the presiding officer, or chairman, who is usually called *speaker*. The lieutenant-governor, in States in which there is one, presides in the senate, and is called *president of the senate*. In the absence of the presiding officer, a temporary speaker or president is chosen, who is called speaker, or president, *pro tempore*, commonly abbreviated *pro tem.*, which is a Latin phrase, meaning *for the time.*

4. **Presiding Officer's Duty.**—The duty of the person presiding is to keep order and to see that the business of the house is conducted according to certain established rules. When a vote is to be taken he puts the question, and when taken he declares the question to be carried or lost. This part of a speaker's business is similar to that of the chairman of an ordinary public meeting.

5. **Minor Officers.**—The other officers chosen by each house are: a *clerk*, to keep a record or journal of its pro-

ceedings, to take charge of papers, etc.; a *sergeant-at-arms*, to arrest members and other persons guilty of disorderly conduct, to compel the attendance of absent members, and to do other business of a like nature; also one or more *door-keepers*. The officers mentioned in this section are not chosen from the members of the house.

6. **Quorum.**—The constitution determines what portion of the members shall constitute a quorum to do business, i.e. how many must be present. *Quorum* is the Latin of the English words *of whom*, and has strangely come to signify the *number* or *portion* of any body of men who have power to act. In most States a majority will constitute a quorum; in some a greater number is required, two thirds or three fifths.

7. **Proceedings Open.**—Constitutions generally require also that the proceedings of legislative bodies shall be open to public inspection. The doors may be closed against spectators only when the public good shall require secrecy. And that the people may be fully informed of what is done, each house is required to keep and publish a journal of its proceedings.

8. **Interruptions.**—Provision is also made, either by the constitution or by law, against injury or interruption to the business of the legislature. Members may not, by any prosecution at law, except for crimes and misdemeanors, be hindered during their attendance at the sessions of the legislature, nor in going to or returning from the same. Each house may compel the attendance of absent members. It may for good cause expel a member and punish not only its members and officers, but other persons, for disorderly conduct or for obstructing its proceedings.

CHAPTER X.

MANNER OF ENACTING LAWS.

1. Power.—The legislature of every State has power to enact any law, on any subject, not forbidden by the Constitution of the United States or its own constitution, and not at variance with any law of Congress. In this particular the extent of its power is broader than that of Congress, for the latter can legislate only on the particular subjects named in the United States Constitution. The subjects which the United States Constitution forbids to the state legislatures will be found in a later chapter (page 155). The state constitutions also contain prohibitions meant to restrain the legislature from making oppressive laws, or such as would endanger the people's absolute rights. (See page 15, § 5.) If any laws are passed contrary to these constitutional provisions, they will be void and of no effect.

2. Rules.—Constitutions prescribe no method of passing laws. They leave it entirely to the legislature itself. But it would be impossible for such a body to act without some order, and so each legislature establishes certain rules, which are seldom departed from. But, though ordinarily followed, these rules may be departed from, and the law will be just as valid, provided a quorum is present and a sufficient number vote for it.

3. Governor's Message.—When the two houses are duly organized and ready for business, the governor sends to both houses a written communication called *a message*, in which, as the constitution requires, he gives to the legislature information of the condition of the affairs of the State, and recommends such measures as he judges necessary and expedient. The message is read to each house by its clerk.

4. Other Measures.—But the measures to which the governor calls the attention of the legislature are but a small portion of those which are considered and acted upon. Many are introduced by individual members. Others are brought into notice by the petitions of the people in different parts of the State. *Petition* generally signifies a request or prayer. As here used, it means a written request to the legislature for some favor—generally for a law granting some benefit or relief to the petitioners. Petitions are sent to members, usually to those who represent the counties or districts in which the petitioners live, and are by these members presented to the house. Laws may be introduced in either house.

5. Committees.—The subjects to be acted on by a legislature are very numerous, and if the whole house carefully examined each measure and listened to all the reasons why the measure was necessary it could not finish half its labor. So committees are appointed at the beginning of the session, consisting of from three to seven members, each committee having charge of some particular subject: such as, the committee on finance, or the money matters of the State, called the ways and means committee; the committee on agriculture; on manufactures; on railroads; on education; and a great many other subjects. As soon as a measure is introduced into the house it is referred to its appropriate committee, to examine into its necessity and report to the house the result of the examination. These committees are so numerous that every member is on at least one or two, and are called *standing committees*, because they continue through the session. When a question arises having no relation to any particular subject on which there is a standing committee, it is usually referred to a *special* or *select* committee appointed to consider this particular matter.

6. Committee Meetings.—Committees meet in private rooms during hours when the house is not in session; and any person wishing to be heard in favor of or against a proposed measure may appear before the committee having it in charge. Having duly considered the subject, the committee reports to the house the information it has obtained, with the opinion whether the measure ought or ought not to become a law. Measures reported against by committees seldom receive any further notice from the house.

7. Bills.—If a committee reports favorably upon a subject, it usually brings in a bill with its report and recommends its passage. A *bill* is the form or draft of a law. Sometimes it is prepared in correct form before it is introduced into the house or referred to the committee. In other cases, as, for instance, when the subject is brought before the house by petition, the committee prepares it.

8. Three Readings.—A bill before it is passed is read three times, on three separate days. In some legislatures the rules allow the first and second readings to be on the same day. The first and second readings consist often of merely reading the title or the enacting clause. Then amendments to it may be introduced, and adopted or rejected. Finally the third reading is had, this time the clerk really reading the bill except where it is a long one, and the final vote is taken. Debate on the bill is not usually had until after the second reading. There are a great many rules covering every point which may arise, such as the order of business, and when debate shall be allowed; and these rules are usually followed: but sometimes, in cases of exigency, all the rules are suspended and a bill is introduced and passed immediately, without being referred to a committee or even being read.

9. Passage.—When the final vote is to be taken, the speaker puts the question: "Shall the bill pass?" If a majority of the members present vote in the affirmative (the speaker also voting), the bill is passed; if a majority vote in the negative, or if the ayes and noes are equal, the bill is lost. In a senate where a lieutenant-governor presides, not being properly a member, he does not vote, except when the ayes and noes are equal, in which case there is said to be a *tie;* and he determines the question by his vote, which is called the *casting* vote. In some States, on the final passage of a bill, a bare majority of the members present is not sufficient to pass it, in case any members are absent. The constitutions of those States require the votes of a majority of *all the members elected* to each house.

10. Other House.—When a bill has passed one house it is sent to the other, where it passes through the same forms of action; that is, it is referred to a committee, reported by the committee to the house, and is read three times before a vote is taken on its passage. This vote having been taken, the bill is returned to the house from which it was received. If it has been amended, the amendments must be agreed to by the first house, or the second must recede from its amendments, or the amendments must be so modified as to secure the approval of both houses, before the bill can become a law.

11. Veto.—But in many of the States a bill, when passed by both houses, is not yet a law. As the two houses may concur in adopting an unwise measure, an additional safeguard is provided against the enactment of bad laws, by requiring all bills to be sent to the governor for examination and approval. If he approves a bill, he signs it, and it is a law; if he does not sign it, it is not a law. In refusing to sign a bill, he is said to *negative* or *veto* the bill. *Veto*, Latin, means *I forbid*.

12. **No Absolute Veto.**—But no governor has full power to prevent the passage of a law. If he does not approve a bill, he must return it to the house in which it originated, stating his objections to it; and if it shall be again passed by both houses, it will be a law without the governor's assent. But in such cases greater majorities are generally required to pass a law. In some States a majority of two thirds of the members present is necessary; in others, a majority of *all the members elected*. In some States if the governor does not return a bill within a certain number of days, it becomes a law without his signature and without being considered a second time.

13. **Taking Effect.**—Laws become operative the minute the last act is done; in those States where the governor must approve them, the minute he signs his name, unless the law itself provides otherwise. But this would often create great hardship, for one might violate a law before he had had time to hear of it. Therefore constitutions often provide that a law shall not take effect for some days after its passage, or the law itself may so provide.

SECTION III.

EXECUTIVE DEPARTMENT.

CHAPTER XI.

STATE OFFICERS.

1. Classification.—The executive officers of a State may be divided into two classes: those whose duties relate to the whole State, as the governor or the attorney-general, and those whose duties relate only to some particular portion of it, as the sheriffs. The first class are elected by all the people of the State, and have their offices at the capital; the latter are elected by the people of the particular district (county, town, or city), and have their offices there. In this chapter we will treat only of the first class.

2. Governor.—The chief executive officer of a State is the governor. In a monarchy the chief executive officer is the monarch himself. But there is this difference: in a monarchy the monarch is the source of power, and all inferior officers are his agents and responsible to him alone; in a republic the people are the source of power, and inferior officers are their agents and responsible to them with the governor, and not to him. He is called the chief officer because he has the highest duties to perform.

3. Term.—The governor is elected by the people, for different terms in the different States. In most States the term is either two or four years; in some New England States it is one year.

4. Qualifications.—The qualifications for the office of governor are also different in the different States. To be eligible, a person must have been for a certain number of years a citizen of the United States, and for a term of years preceding his election a resident of the State. He must also be above a certain age, which in a majority of the States is thirty years; and in some States he must own a certain amount of property.

5. Executive Powers.—The governor's executive powers and duties are numerous and important. He represents the State in its dealings with other States. He is commander-in-chief of the military force of the State, and can call it out in times of insurrection. He is to take care that the laws are faithfully executed, and may require information at any time from the different executive officers concerning the condition of affairs in their respective departments. He communicates by message to the legislature, at every session, information of the condition of the State, and recommends such measures as he judges necessary and expedient. He may convene the legislature on extraordinary occasions; that is, when some important matter arises requiring immediate attention.

6. Legislative Powers.—In most States the governor has the veto power. (See page 43, § 11.)

7. Judicial Powers.—A governor has power to grant reprieves and pardons, except in cases of impeachment, and, in some States, of treason. To *reprieve* is to postpone or delay for a time the execution of the sentence of death upon a criminal. To *pardon* is to annul the sentence by forgiving the offence and releasing the offender. A governor may also *commute* a sentence, which is to exchange one penalty or punishment for another of less severity; as, when a person sentenced to suffer death is ordered to be imprisoned.

8. Appointments.—The governor also appoints some executive or judicial officers. The power of appointment varies greatly in the different States: in some he appoints all the higher executive and judicial officers, such as the secretary of state, the attorney-general, or the judges of the courts; in others, those are all elected, and he only appoints some lower officers, such as notaries. He almost never has the power to appoint legislative officers. He also fills vacancies in executive and judicial offices, until the next election, when they occur through death or resignation. He has in some cases the power of removal for misconduct.

These are only the principal powers and duties devolved on the governor. He has many others.

9. Councils.—In a few States an *executive council* is elected by the people, whose duty it is to advise the governor. In many cases, as, for instance, appointments, he must obtain their consent.

10. Lieutenant-Governor.—In many of the States this office does not exist.* He has few duties. In most States where the office exists, he presides in the senate, in which he has only a casting vote. The chief object of this office seems to be to provide a suitable person to fill the vacancy in the office of governor in case the latter should die, resign, be removed, or otherwise become incompetent.

11. Assistant Officers.—Among the executive officers who assist in the administration of the government, there are in every State some or all of the following: a secretary of state, a comptroller or auditor, a treasurer, and an attorney-general. In some States they are appointed by the governor, in others by the legislature, and in others they are elected by the people.

12. The Secretary of State has charge of the State papers and records. He keeps a record of the official acts

---

* Viz:. Alabama, Arkansas, Delaware, Georgia, Maine, Maryland, New Hamps[   ]a.

and proceedings of the legislature and of the executive departments, and has the care of the books, records, deeds of the State, parchments, the laws enacted by the legislature, and all other papers and documents required by law to be kept in his office.

13. **The State Comptroller,** in some States called *auditor*, manages the financial concerns of the State; that is, the business relating to the money, debts, land, and other property of the State. He examines and adjusts accounts and claims against the State, and superintends the collection of moneys due the State. When money is to be paid out he draws a warrant on the state treasurer.

14. **The State Treasurer** has charge of all the moneys of the State, and pays out the same as directed by law, and keeps an accurate account of such moneys.

15. **Official Bonds.**—Auditors, treasurers, and other officers intrusted with the care and management of money or other property are generally required, before they enter on the duties of their offices, to give bonds, in sums of certain amount specified in the law, with sufficient sureties, for the faithful performance of their duties. The sureties are persons who sign the bond with the officer, and bind themselves to pay the State all damages arising from neglect of duty on the part of the officer, not exceeding the sum mentioned in the bond.

16. **The Attorney-General** is a lawyer who acts for the State in lawsuits in which the State is a party. He prosecutes persons indebted to the State, and causes to be brought to trial persons charged with certain crimes. He also gives his opinion on questions of law submitted to him by the governor, the legislature, and the executive officers.

17. **Other Officers.**—There are also in some States the following officers: a *surveyor-general,* who superintends

the surveying of the lands belonging to the State, and who keeps in his office maps describing the bounds of the counties and townships; a *superintendent of schools* or *superintendent of public instruction,* who attends to many matters connected with the public schools of the State; a *state printer,* who prints the laws and all state papers; a *state librarian,* who has charge of the state library; and others.

CHAPTER XII.

COUNTY OFFICERS.

1. Reasons for Division.—A State is divided into counties,* and each county is divided into towns.† Thus every part of the State is within some town and some county. There are several reasons for this division: for convenience in the legislative, executive, and judicial departments. Some laws may be necessary in some parts of the State that are not needed in others, and which the people of those parts can better make for themselves, and the boun-

---

* Counties in the same State are about the same size, and have about the same population; but the counties of one State as compared with those of another vary very greatly as to number, size, and population. In 1870, Massachusetts had 14 counties, Texas 162, and Oregon 25; in Massachusetts there were about 500 square miles in a county, in Texas 1500, and in Oregon 4000; in Massachusetts the population in a county was about 100,000, in Texas 5000, and in Oregon 4000. Counties exist in every State except Louisiana.

† Towns or townships also vary in size, but perhaps a fair average would be from five to ten miles square. Towns do not exist, generally, in the Southern States or the extreme Western States. There the county is not divided except for special purposes.

daries must be clearly fixed that it may be known who comes under the regulations or who can make them. So, too, there are many executive officers, such as sheriffs and collectors of taxes, but each must have his jurisdiction confined to particular limits or there would be great confusion. There are many lower courts, too, and the jurisdiction of each must be clearly defined.

2. Origin of County.—Counties in England were formerly districts governed by *counts* or earls, from which comes the name of *county*. A county was also called *shire*, and an officer was appointed by the count or earl to perform certain acts in the principal town in the county, which was called *shire town*, and the officer was called *shire-reeve*, or *sheriff*. He was a more important officer than the sheriff of a county in this country now is. The court-house and other county buildings are situated at the principal place in the county, and it is called the *county-seat*, or *capital*.

3. Political Importance.—In the Southern and extreme Western States the county is the most important political division, and exercises most of the local governmental powers, such as many important powers with regard to the establishment of common schools, regulation of roads, laying and collection of taxes, care of the poor, etc. In New England the town exercises most of these powers, and the county has very little importance. In the remainder—that is, in the Middle and Western States (except those far west)—these powers are divided between the county and town.

4. Corporations.—Counties, towns, cities, and villages are *municipal corporations*. Let us see what a corporation is. Persons, in a legal sense, are divided into two classes, *natural persons* and *corporations*. Natural Persons are human beings, as God made them; Corporations are artificial persons, or bodies, created by law. In other words, a *corporation* (also called *a body politic*, or *body corporate*) is an association of persons authorized by law to transact business under a common name and as a single person. The laws of the State give such authority to the inhabitants of counties and towns. The people of a town or county have power, to some extent, to buy, hold, and sell property, and sue and be sued, as single individuals. Therefore they are corporations. So, also, is the State itself. But there are two kinds of corporations: *public*, or *municipal*, and *private*. Public, or municipal corporations are those organized for purposes of government, such as counties, towns, cities, and villages; private corporations are all others, such as banks, railroad companies, and churches.

5. County Commissioners.—We have seen that a county is a corporation, and that corporations have power to act as single persons. But a corporation must act by means of natural persons, i.e. by its agents. The chief agent of a county—that is, the body which exercises the most important corporate powers—is a board of *county commissioners* (usually three). In a few States these powers are exercised by and in the name of the *board of supervisors*, which is composed of the supervisors of the several towns in the county, of whom there is one supervisor in each town. These boards have charge of the county property, and may make orders and contracts in relation to the building or repairing of the court-house, jail, and other county buildings. In those States in which the county exercises more political power than the town, these boards have many powers with regard to schools, roads, taxes, etc. The following are the more important county officers which exist in every State:

6. County Treasurer.—There is in each county a *treasurer* to receive and pay out the moneys of the county, as required. There is also, in some States, a county *auditor* to examine and adjust the accounts and debts of the county. The business of county treasurers and auditors in their respective counties is of the same nature as that of state auditors and treasurers, and they are required to give bonds in the same way. In States in which there is no county auditor, the duties of auditor are performed by the treasurer.

7. Recorder.—There is also in each county a *register* or *recorder*, who records in books provided for that purpose all deeds, mortgages, and other instruments of writing required by law to be recorded. In New York and in some other States the business of a register or recorder is done by a county clerk, who is also clerk of the several courts held in the county. In some States deeds, mortgages, and other written instruments are recorded by the town clerks of the several towns.

8. Sheriff.—Another county officer is a *sheriff*, whose duty it is to execute all warrants, writs, and other process directed to him by the courts; to apprehend persons charged with crime; and to take charge of the jail and of the prisoners therein. It is his duty, also, to preserve the public peace; and he may cause all persons who break the public peace within his knowledge or view to give bonds, with sureties, for keeping the peace and for appearing at the next court to be held in the county, and to commit them to jail if they refuse to give such bonds. A sheriff is assisted by deputies.

9. Coroner.—There are in each county one or more *coroners*, whose principal duty is to inquire into the cause of the death of persons who have died by violence, or suddenly, and by means unknown. Notice of the death of a person having so died is given to a coroner, who institutes an examination. A jury is summoned to attend the examination; witnesses are examined; and the jury give their opinion in writing as to the cause and manner of the death. Such inquiry is called a *coroner's inquest.*

10. The District Attorney is a lawyer who attends all courts in the county in which persons are tried for crimes, and conducts the prosecution. As all crimes and breaches of the peace are considered as committed against the State, and prosecuted in its name, this attorney is sometimes called *state's attorney,* or *prosecuting attorney.*

11. Other Officers.—There are often other officers in each county; such as, *assessors,* who assess the value of each one's property so that it may be known what tax he shall pay; *collectors of taxes;* a *county surveyor;* a *superintendent of schools.*

12. Elected.—County officers are generally elected by the people of the county, for terms of from one to four years. Some of them are, in some of the States, appointed by some authority prescribed by the constitution or laws of the State.

13. Whom They Represent.—While the different county officers are alike in this respect, that their jurisdiction extends only to their particular county, and also in this fact, that in their official acts they act as representatives or agents of the people; they differ from each other in this, that while some represent the people of the whole State (and in that sense may be called state officers), others represent only the people of their own county. Thus, when a sheriff arrests a man for crime, it is the State which arrests him by the hand of its agent in that county; when the district attorney prosecutes him, it is the State which is trying him for the crime against itself. (See page 80, footnote.) On the other hand the county commissioners commonly act only as agents of their county. Some officers may represent the State in some of their duties. and the county :

CHAPTER XIII.

TOWN OFFICERS.

1. Towns.—In all the States except those far west and most of the Southern States, each county is subdivided. These subdivisions are called *towns* at the East, and *townships* at the West and South. At the West and South a village or city is often called a town. But in this book we shall use the word *town* as meaning an organized subdivision of a county. In those States where towns do not exist, the county exercises all the local governmental powers and has all the necessary officers. It must be remembered, then, that this chapter does not apply to all the States.

2. Chief Officer.—Since a town is a corporation, it must, like a county, have some one to represent it and act for it. The principal officer, or board, whose duty this is has different names in different States. In the New England towns there are what are called *selectmen*, three or more in each town. In a few States there are *trustees of townships*. In a few other States there is in each town one such officer, called *supervisor*. The powers and duties of these officers are the most numerous and important in New England, where the town is the most important division of the State. They have duties with regard to taking charge of the town property, laying out and repairing roads, collecting taxes, providing for the poor, etc. In those States where the county is the more important division, the town officers have fewer of these duties, and the county officers have mor

3. Treasurer.—There is often a *town treasurer*, with duties, in his own town, analogous to those of a county treasurer.

4. Town Clerk.—A *town clerk* in each town keeps the records, books, and papers of the town. He records in a book the proceedings of town meetings, the names of the persons elected, and such other papers as are required by law to be recorded.

5. Constables.—There are several *constables* in each town. Their principal duties are to serve all writs and processes issued by justices of the peace. The business of a constable in executing the orders of a justice of the peace is similar to that of a sheriff in relation to the county courts.

6. Highways.—For the repairing of *highways and bridges*, a town is divided by the proper officers into as many road districts as may be judged convenient; and a person residing in each district is chosen, called *overseer* or *supervisor*, or *surveyor* of *highways*, whose duty it is to see that the roads and bridges are repaired and kept in order in his district. In some cases a tax is laid for the purpose, and ordinary laborers do the work. In others, each one taxed may work on the road himself a certain number of days, or he may pay the tax, according as he wishes.

7. Overseers of the Poor provide for the support of paupers belonging to the town, who have no near relatives able to support them. In some States there is in each county a poor-house, to which the paupers of the several towns are sent to be provided for; the expense to be charged to the towns to which such poor persons belonged.

8. Other Officers.—There are often in every town other inferior officers: *assessors* and *collectors of taxes* (see Chap.

XV.); certain *school-officers; fence-viewers*, who settle disputes as to division fences; *pound-keepers*, who take charge of stray animals; *sealers*, who keep correct copies of the standard of weights and measures; and others.

9. Elected.—Most town officers are elected by the electors of their respective towns at the annual town meetings, for terms of one year.

10. Town Meetings.—These are meetings of the electors held once a year in every town for the election of town officers and for certain other business. They exist only in New England and a few other States which have been under the influence of New England. At them the people not only elect officers, but take some share in the government. For instance, they have power to vote what money shall be raised for school purposes, for highways, and other purposes; what salaries shall be paid different officers; what proceedings shall be taken at law; and other powers. This, as far as it goes, is pure democracy. With a county it is different. The people of a county never meet together except to elect officers, and take no part, directly, in the direction of affairs.

CHAPTER XIV.

CITIES AND VILLAGES.

1. Reasons for Incorporation.—A city, or a village,* is a particular portion of a town which has become so thickly populated that a different kind of government is needed

---

* The word *village* very often means only a collection of houses, or of people living near one another, but in this chapter we shall use the word for an *incorporated village*. In Connecticut and Pennsylvania an inc

from that of the rest of the town. For instance, where there are many people who use the streets, sidewalks will be necessary, and where the houses are near to each other, as in the ordinary village, fire-engines and fire-companies will be necessary to prevent the whole place from being destroyed; and if the population is still more dense, as in a city, many other regulations are necessary—such as, with regard to police, water supply, cleaning the streets, sewers, etc. But towns do not have the power to regulate these things. It is thought best that the people living in those thickly populated portions should do it themselves. The legislature of the State gives them these powers by *incorporating* them into a village or city.

2. **Charter.**—Whenever, therefore, the inhabitants of any portion of a town become so numerous as to require a government with more powers than the rest of the town, they petition the legislature for a law incorporating them into a village, or, if they are very numerous, a city. The law or act of incorporation is usually called a *charter*. The word *charter* is from the Latin *charta*, which means paper. The instruments of writing by which kings or other sovereign powers granted rights and privileges to individuals or corporations were written on paper or parchment, and called *charters*. In this country it is commonly used to designate an act of the legislature conferring privileges and powers upon cities, villages, and other corporations.

3. **Its Contents.**—The charter describes the boundaries of the city and village, prescribes what officers it shall have, and what shall be their powers and duties.

4. **City Officers.**—The chief executive officer of a city is a *mayor*. A city is divided into wards of convenient size, in each of which are chosen one or more *aldermen* (usually two) and such other officers as are named in the charter.

The mayor and aldermen constitute the *city council*, which is a kind of legislature, having the power to pass such laws (commonly called *ordinances*) as the government of the city requires.* There are also elected in the several wards assessors, constables, collectors, and other necessary officers, whose duties in their respective wards are similar to those of like-named officers in country towns, or townships.

5. Village Officers.—The chief executive officer of a village is, in some States, called *president*. The village is not divided into wards, the number of its inhabitants being too small to require such division. Instead of a board of aldermen there is a board of *trustees* or *directors*, who exercise similar powers. The president of a village is generally chosen by the trustees from their own number. In some States incorporated villages are called *towns*, and their chief executive officer is called *mayor*.

6. General Law.—The constitutions of some States require the legislature to pass a general law prescribing the manner in which the people in any place may form themselves into an incorporated village without a special law or charter.

7. Subject to Laws of State.—The inhabitants of cities and villages, however, are not governed alone by laws made by the common council and the trustees. Those laws and regulations relate only to local matters. Most of the laws enacted by the legislature are of general application, and have the same effect in cities and villages as elsewhere. Thus the laws of the State require that taxes shall be assessed and levied upon the property of the citizens of the State to defray the public expenses, and the

---

* In some cases there are two boards, in analogy with the two legislative houses of the State.

Executive Department.

people of the cities are required to pay their just proportion of the same; but the city authorities lay and collect additional taxes for city purposes.

8. Corporations.—We have seen that the State, counties, towns, cities, and villages are all corporations, and that there are also other corporations, such as banks, railroad companies, etc. Now all corporations are alike in some particulars. They all continue after the persons first composing them are dead. They all have power to

DIAGRAM SHOWING THE RELATION BETWEEN COUNTY, TOWN, CITY, AND VILLAGE.

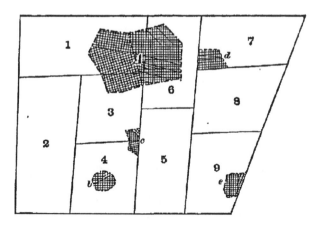

The whole diagram represents a county.
The numbers represent the towns into which it is divided.
A represents a city.
b, c, d, and e represent villages.

buy and sell property, and to borrow money to a certain extent. But they also differ in some respects. A State differs from other municipal corporations in the manner of formation. A State is formed by the people when they adopt the constitution; the other municipal corporations —i.e. cities, towns, etc.—are formed by the legislature. Again, all municipal corporations differ from other corporations in two particulars: their purpose and their membership. Municipal corporations are organized only for purposes of government; the others are organized for other purposes, such as business (banks, insurance companies, etc.), religion (churches), or charity (hospitals, etc.). Of a municipal corporation every one is a member who lives within its limits, whether he wishes to be or not; but in other corporations one only becomes a member by his own choice.

CHAPTER XV.

TAXES.

1. Reasons for Them.—Every government must have the power of providing means for its support. The different state, county, and town officers must be paid salaries; money is needed for public buildings, such as state-houses, court-houses, jails, etc.; and there are other necessities. The money which is needed to pay the expenses of administering the government, if the State, county, or town has no permanent source of revenue or income, must be raised by taxation. A *tax* is a sum of money assessed upon the person of a citizen for the use of the government. When each one is required to pay a certain sum, the same for all, it is called a *poll-tax*, or *capitation tax*, being a certain sum on every poll, or head. But, as persons ought to contribute to the public expenses according to their ability, taxes are more just when laid upon the citizens in proportion to the property each one owns. In ordinary speech we say that the property itself is taxed.

2. Land Tax most Common.—Both real and personal property* are subject to taxation; but in the United States most of the taxes are laid upon the land, for the reason that it is always difficult for the assessors to ascertain all the personal property each one owns. Poll-taxes are laid in many States, but they are very small.

3. Assessment.—This means valuation. As every person is to be taxed in proportion to the value of his property, it is necessary, first, to make a correct valuation of all his taxable property. For this purpose, the assessor or assessors pass through the town, and make a list of the names of all the taxable inhabitants, and the estimated value of the property, real and personal, of each. If any one thinks his property is valued at too high a rate, he has an opportunity to appear before the assessors and ask to have the assessment reduced. The town assessors then make returns to the proper state and county officers of all the property, and its valuation, in the town.

4. Information.—In some States persons liable to taxation are themselves required to furnish lists of all their taxable property, printed blank lists having been previously distributed among them for this purpose. To secure an accurate valuation, the assessors (called also *listers*) may require persons to make oath that they have made a true statement of their property and its value.

5. Exemptions.—There are certain kinds of property which are exempt from taxation; such as the corporate

---

* *Real estate*, or *real property*, is land with the buildings and other articles erected or growing thereon. *Personal estate*, or *personal property*, is every other kind of property; such as, goods, stocks and bonds, money, and debts due from debtors.

property of the State, of counties, and of towns, including the buildings in which the public business is done, the prisons, jails, asylums, etc., and the lands attached to them; school-houses and churches, with the lands attached; burying-grounds, and the property of literary and charitable institutions. But the property of business corporations, as railroad, banking, insurance, manufacturing, and other stock companies, like that of individuals, is liable to taxation.

6. Three Amounts.—Before a tax-list can be made out, showing what each one's tax is to be, it must be known what amount is to be collected in each town. This amount is made up of three parts: first, the sum wanted to pay the expenses of the town for the current year; second, the town's share of the county expenses; and third, its proportionate share of the expenses of the state government, or of what is to be raised for state purposes. In this country the amount that each one pays for state purposes is usually very much less than what he pays for county and town purposes. The ratio of the county to the town tax varies in proportion to the political importance of the county and town. In many States there is no town tax.

7. Apportionment.—The apportionment of the amount of the state and county expenses among the several towns is made according to the amount of property in each as valued by the assessors. The state auditor or comptroller having received from the several counties returns of the value of the property in each county, is enabled to determine its quota of the amount to be raised for state purposes. He sends to the proper officers in each county (county commissioners, or board of supervisors) a statement showing what part of the state tax the county is to pay. The county officers add to each county's share of the state expenses the sum to be raised in the county for county purposes, and apportion the whole amount among the towns in proportion to the value of the property in each. Then the town officers, in turn, add to each town's share of the amount of the state and county expenses the amount to be raised for town purposes, and this gives the whole sum to be collected in the town. This sum is divided up among the inhabitants of the town in proportion to their property as valued by the assessors, and a tax-list, showing what each one is to pay, is given to the collector. In cities and villages each one's tax includes also his proportionate share of the amount to be raised for city, or village, purposes. Taxes in cities are usually very much higher than anywhere else.

8. **Collection.**—When the collector has received the taxes he pays them over to the town treasurer. The latter retains the portion collected for town purposes, and remits the remainder to his county treasurer. The county treasurer retains the portion collected for county purposes and remits the remainder to the state treasurer. The system of assessment and collection of taxes varies in the different States. The system described in this chapter applies chiefly to the Northern States.

9. **Tax Sales.**—Where a person neglects to pay his tax, means are provided by law to enforce payment. If he is taxed for personal property, sometimes the collector may seize his goods and sell them, and sometimes suit must be brought in the usual way. But if he is taxed for land, a different course is pursued. In a certain sense, the land itself is taxed. If the tax is not paid within a certain time, the proper authorities sell or lease the land for a certain period to any one who will pay the tax. The owner then has the right to redeem within a certain time, generally two or three years, by paying to the purchaser what he has paid for taxes, with interest. The purchaser does not

have the right to take possession of the land until the time to redeem has expired.

10. Assessments.—*Assessment* has been used in the sense of valuation. But it is also often used to mean a tax laid in a city to pay for some public improvement; such as, the building of a sewer, the paving of a street, the laying out of a park, etc. In such cases the benefit of the improvement is felt, sometimes wholly, generally chiefly, by those who live near, and therefore they are required to pay for it. For instance, when a sewer is built in a side street, only the property on each side of that street is assessed for it.

11. Indirect Taxes.—The taxes that have been described are called *direct taxes*. But there are also *indirect taxes*, so called because, when finally paid, they are not paid directly to the government as a tax, but as a part of the price of something. They include duties which are paid on goods exported from a country or imported into it, on goods manufactured, licenses for carrying on certain trades, or for doing certain things, etc. For instance, if a tax is laid on the manufacture of liquors, the manufacturer adds enough to the price of the liquor to cover the tax, and so the consumer, when he buys, indirectly pays the tax. Only a small portion of the revenue of a State is derived from indirect taxation. The United States Constitution forbids any State to lay import or export duties.

CHAPTER XVI.

EDUCATION.

1. A Proper Object of Government.—The proper object of government is to promote the welfare and happiness of its citizens. For this purpose it must protect the people in the enjoyment of life and the fruits of their labor. But it should go further, and make express provision for improving the condition of the people, especially the less fortunate portions of them. The prosperity of a State or nation depends essentially upon the education of its citizens. Ignorance tends to make men idle and vicious. On the other hand, education not only teaches them better ways of living, but impels them to follow the better ways, and gives them higher purposes in life.

2. A Political Necessity.—But further, we believe that a government by the people is better adapted than any other to promote the general welfare where the people are fitted to govern. But if the people are not properly educated, they are incapable of self-government. Some children are educated at private schools. But very many are unable to pay for the education of their children in that way, and therefore each State has established a system of *common schools*, at which the children of all may be taught at the public expense. These are the schools we shall treat of in this chapter. It is to its common-school system that the United States owes much of its prosperity as a nation. This system has been developed more highly at the North than at the South. But the constitutions adopted in the Southern States since the late civil war have made much more adequate provision for this necessity than existed in those States previously.

3. **Support.**—The schools are supported chiefly by taxation. In some cases those who send their children there have to pay a higher rate than others. But in almost all the States there is provided a school fund, the income from which is applied to aid in their support. A *fund* is a sum of money, the income from which is set apart for a particular purpose. Thus the interest of a school fund is applied in building school-houses, paying teachers, etc. The whole amount expended on common schools in the United States in 1870 was about $64,000,000.

4. **Creation of School Funds.**—These were created in the older States by the State's appropriating certain lands owned by it to that purpose. They were, in many cases, largely increased by certain moneys received from the United States. In 1836 there had accumulated in the national treasury about thirty millions of dollars over and above what was needed for the support of the government. By an act of Congress, this surplus revenue was distributed among the States then existing, to be kept by them until called for by Congress. That it never will be called for is now almost certain. Many of the States have appropriated large portions of their respective shares for school purposes. From its having been said to be only *deposited* with the States, this fund is sometimes called the *United States deposit fund*. As to the Western States, at an early period, while most of the territory from which they have been formed was yet the property of the United States, and uninhabited, Congress passed acts by which a certain proportion of the land in every township is reserved for the support of schools therein. By these acts, in some of those States one thirty-sixth, in others one eighteenth of the whole State has been thus appropriated, besides smaller portions

granted for the benefit of a university in each State. In States which may be hereafter formed out of existing territories, land will be reserved in the same way. The whole amount of the permanent common-school funds in the United States in 1872 was calculated to be about $65,000,-000. The income from this is applied to school purposes every year.

5. Districts.—The towns, or townships, of a State are generally divided into districts of proper size, in each one of which is established a school, to which all the children of the district may go, free of expense. These schools are sometimes called *district schools,* sometimes *common schools,* and sometimes *public schools.* Each district has apportioned to it its share of the income of the school fund, and the rest of the money needed to support the school is raised from the inhabitants of the district or the State by taxation. One or more *trustees* or *directors* are chosen in each district to manage the school affairs.

6. State Superintendent.—In many States there is an officer called the *state superintendent of public schools,* or *superintendent of public instruction.* The superintendent collects information relating to the schools; the number of children residing in each district and the number taught; the number of school-houses, and the amount yearly expended; and other matters concerning the operation and effects of the common-school system. Sometimes he also apportions the money arising from the state funds among the several counties. He reports to the legislature at every session the information he has collected, and suggests such improvements in the school system as he thinks ought to be made. There are officers in each county or town to aid him in this work. There are also officers in each county or town who examine the teachers periodically to see if they are competent.

7. Grades.—Public schools are divided into three grades: *primary* schools, for the youngest pupils; *grammar* schools, in which are taught, besides the ordinary, some of the higher, branches of study; and *high* schools, for the most advanced, in which are taught the studies necessary for a business education, and frequently the languages and higher mathematics. But it is only in the largest places that the higher grades exist. Many contend that the public should not be taxed to furnish a higher education, but that it should be left to the private citizen. Others maintain that the general good demands that some should be highly educated. But, though many States have high schools, universities, and other educational institutions, supported or aided by the State, the great body of schools in the country still are of the lower grade.

8. Compulsory Attendance.—In general, the State does not compel parents to send their children to school, but relies upon their own sense of duty and interest. But in a few States it does, and every child is compelled to go to some school, public or private, a certain portion of every year between the ages of seven and fourteen. And the idea is gaining strength in the country that the interest of the whole people requires that every child should be educated to a certain degree.

9. Normal Schools.—These are schools in which persons are trained to be teachers. If a State is to furnish education to its citizens, it must provide suitable educators, and therefore most States have established one or more of these schools. They are free to any one, but in return the person taught must serve a certain length of time (two or three years) as a teacher in the common schools of the State. In that way he pays for his education.

CHAPTER XVII.

PUBLIC INSTITUTIONS.

1. Duty of Government.—We have seen that a government ought to provide means not only for the protection of the lives and property of its citizens, but also for their education. But there are further duties which it owes to its citizens. It ought to furnish protection and aid to those who are unfortunate, the insane, the blind, orphan children, and others who are unable to care for themselves. So, too, if there is any great enterprise in which all the people of the State are interested, but which is too large or too costly to be carried on by private individuals, the State should render aid. Again, a State should exercise some control over the operations of corporations having large powers, such as railroads and banks, in order to prevent fraud upon the people. These duties are important functions of the executive department.

2. Asylums.—Every State establishes and supports some of these for the insane, blind, deaf and dumb, inebriate, orphans, and others. At them support and medical aid is furnished to such as have no means of providing for themselves. Counties, towns, and cities often maintain institutions of the same kind.

3. Canals.—These do not exist in all the States, and in some they are constructed and managed by private corporations. But in others they are state works, built by the State and managed by officers elected by the people. New York, Pennsylvania, and Ohio have many. Their object is to furnish cheap transportation, and at one time they were considered of vast importance, but railroads have in a great measure taken their place. Where the State undertakes such an enterprise, very often a fund is provided by the State the income of which is applied to the object, and the United States increases this fund by grants to it of public lands, because the canal is a benefit not only to the people of the State, but also to all the people of the Nation.

4. **Railroads.**—These are seldom state works, but they often receive aid from the State in the form of money lent them, public land granted to them, or state guaranties of their bonds. In a certain other respect all railroads are aided by the State. The property which a railroad company requires very often cannot be purchased, as the owners will not sell, and no person or corporation has, in itself, the right to compel them to sell. But a State has the right to take any one's property for public use on paying its value. This is called the right of *eminent domain*, and this right the State delegates to the railroad company for the time being. Appraisers are appointed who value the land, and on payment of that price the company takes it. The land necessary for a canal is acquired in the same way.

5. **Control of Corporations.**—The State generally exercises some control over certain corporations which, like railway or canal companies, banks, and insurance companies, have large powers and privileges. This is to prevent their being used to the fraud and injury of the public. In some States there are departments, such as the *bank department*, or the *insurance department*, all subordinate branches of the executive department, which are required to exercise supervision over the corporations belonging to their department within the State. They collect information with regard to them, their property and business, by means of examinations and of annual reports which the cor-

porations are required to make, and this information is published. When state banks issued bills (which were only their promises to pay money), they were often required to deposit a certain amount of property with the State to secure those who used their bills as money against loss. So, too, insurance companies are sometimes required to make deposits with the government to secure their policy-holders. There are other ways in which a State exercises control over corporations.

6. State-Prisons.—These are prisons maintained by the State, in which criminals convicted of the higher crimes are confined. The county jails and penitentiaries are for the lower grades of criminals. Convicts are forced to work while confined. In many States their labor is leased by the State to certain contractors, who pay the State as for so many laborers. Thus state-prisons are sometimes rendered self-supporting.

7. State Debts.—Very often the public works undertaken by a State require more money than can be conveniently raised at once by taxation. So, too, perhaps the chief benefit is going to accrue, not to people living at the time the work is done, but many years later, and therefore posterity should bear some share of the burden. In such case the State borrows the money and issues its bonds for it, also called *state stock*. Counties, towns, and cities, in the same way, often incur debt and issue bonds for public works. But there is this difference: counties, towns, and cities may be sued in the courts, but there is no way for a private individual to force a State to pay its debts. Such refusal to pay is called *repudiation*, and several of the States have repudiated their debts in part. For the reason that there is no remedy, repudiation is the more dishonorable. In the late Civil War the Southern States contracted large debts, but these the United States Constitution forbids them to pay. No government could recognize as just, or allow to be paid, if it could prevent it, any debts incurred in a rebellion against it.

CHAPTER XVIII.
MILITIA.

1. Meaning of Militia.—Every nation has its military force to resist foreign enemies and crush rebellion. It consists of two portions, the *standing army* and the *militia*. The standing army is all the time organized, equipped, and drilled, and its members have no other occupation. The militia consists of all the other able-bodied men in the nation (between certain ages), but it is not called into service except in time of war or insurrection. In this country the Nation has a small standing army, and its militia consists of the militia of all the States. The States have no standing army, but each has its militia.

2. Of Whom Composed.—The militia of a State consists of all able-bodied male citizens of the United States between the ages of eighteen and forty-five years who reside in the State, except such as are exempt by the laws of the States and of the United States. Persons exempt by the laws of the State are generally members of the state legislative, executive, and judicial departments, clergymen, teachers, physicians, firemen, and members of military companies who have served a certain time.* Persons

---

* In many States those, also, are exempt who have conscientious scruples as to whether war is ever right, such as the Quakers.

exempt by United States laws are members of the national legislative, executive, and judicial departments, pilots, mariners, and a few others.

3. Commander-in-Chief.—By the constitutions of the several States, the governors are made the commanders-in-chief of the militia of their respective States. The governor has power to call it out in time of insurrection or rebellion,* and when called out he exercises the usual powers of commander over it. He cannot, however, send any member out of the State without his own consent.

4. Organization.—The militia, when organized, is divided in the usual way into brigades, regiments, companies, etc., with the usual officers: adjutant-general, colonels, captains, etc. In some States the officers are appointed by the governor or the legislature; in others they are elected by the men they are to command. But in most of the States the militia remains practically unorganized.

5. Training.—For many years after the Revolution, when the militia was more or less organized all the time, it was called out annually in each State for the purpose of training; but these annual trainings were seen to be of so little value that they gradually fell into disuse. At present the militia in this country is not much more, practically, than an imaginary body, and the great body of the people have no military duties to perform.

6. Volunteer Regiments.—But occasions do arise when it is necessary for a State to have some organized, equipped, and drilled force at hand. This necessity is supplied by the volunteer companies, or regiments, existing in most of the

---

* An *insurrection* is an attempt of persons to prevent the execution of a law. *Rebellion* generally means nearly the same; but more properly it signifies a revolt, or an attempt to overthrow the government to establish a different one.

States. These organize themselves, elect their own members and officers, select their own uniform, and the branch of the service to which they will attach themselves. The State usually grants them more or less aid, in the way of arms, armories, etc. When organized, they come under the military laws of the State, and subject to the orders of the commander-in-chief, in the same manner as the militia is, and he can call them out when necessary. These regiments are called in some States the *national guard*, and popularly they are called the *militia*.

7. United States Militia.—We have said the militia of the United States consisted of the militia of all the States. The President has power to call it out at times when the standing army is not sufficient, and when so called out it passes out of state control and under that of the United States. But this refers to the unorganized militia. Over the volunteer regiments spoken of in the preceding section the United States has no control. It is not probable that the unorganized militia will ever be called out by the national government, but that the latter, like the States, will rely on the formation of volunteer regiments when the necessity arises. In the late Civil War most of the United States army was composed of volunteer regiments formed in the loyal States, and then mustered into the United States service.

SECTION IV.

JUDICIAL DEPARTMENT.

CHAPTER XIX.

COURTS.

1. Necessity.—The judicial department consists of the courts of a State. We have seen that the legislative department makes laws and the executive department carries them out; but there is one other function of government which properly comes in between the making and the execution of the law. This is its application to particular cases when disputes arise. Very often in a particular case it will be hard to tell what the truth is, as one party will say one thing and the other another; and again one side will claim that the law does not include his case, and the other side will claim that it does. These points must be decided before the law can be executed. The executive department might decide them, but justice is more likely to be done if the one that decides has nothing else to do with the case. For this reason the separate judicial department is established. The higher courts of a State are usually established by its constitution, the lower courts by the legislature.

2. Diversity.—There is great diversity among the States in the names and powers of the different courts. No two States are exactly alike. But the following sketch gives a general idea of the judicial system prevailing in most of the States.

3. Court for the Trial of Impeachments.—This is the name applied to the upper house of the legislature when trying a public officer for malfeasance (i.e. corrupt conduct) in office.* *Impeachment* is the formal act of the lower house by which it makes the charge against him.† Generally the lower house has the sole right of impeachment, and the upper house the sole right to try impeachments. On such trial the upper house is in reality a court.‡

4. Supreme Court.—This is the name usually given to the highest court—of which there is only one—in the State. It consists of several judges (very often three), and has usually only appellate jurisdiction.§ Appeals may be taken to it in both civil and criminal cases,‖ from the next lower—the Circuit—courts.

---

* As, if a governor, for money offered him, should approve and sign a law; or a judge should, for money or from some other selfish or personal motive, give a wrong judgment.

† It must be remembered that impeachment is not the conviction of the offence, but only the accusation. It is analogous to an indictment by a grand jury. (See page 84.) It may happen, therefore, that an officer is impeached and afterward acquitted on the trial, as President Andrew Johnson was in 1868.

‡ This practice has come from Great Britain, where the impeachment is made by the House of Commons, and the House of Lords is the High Court of Impeachment.

§ The word *jurisdiction* is from the Latin *jus*, law, and *dictio*, a pronouncing or speaking. Hence the *jurisdiction* of a court means the class of cases in which it has power to pronounce the law. A court is said to have *original* jurisdiction when the case may originate (be commenced) in it; it has *appellate* jurisdiction when it may hear the case on appeal from a lower court.

‖ *Civil* cases are those between private parties for debt or for some injury to person or property. *Criminal* cases are those in which the State seeks to punish one for some criminal offence.

Judicial Department. 77

5. **Circuit Courts.***— Of these there are generally a number (from ten to thirty) in every State, one for each district into which the State is divided. In many States they are called *district courts*, because there is one in each district; in a few they correspond to the *superior* courts, so called because they are of higher grade than the justices' courts. They have original jurisdiction, in general, of all classes of cases, both civil and criminal, and are the courts in which the great body of trials are had. They also hear appeals from the lower courts.

6. **Justices of the Peace.**—In each town, or similar division, there are usually several of these officers. Each justice holds court, and has power to try civil cases which involve small amounts (in some States it must be less than $100, in others less than $50), and to try persons who have committed small offences. They also have important powers with regard to arresting and examining those accused of higher crimes. (See page 85.) In many States, also, they have executive duties.

7. **Probate Courts.**—There is usually one of these in every county, composed of a single judge. They are quite different in character from the courts already described. Their powers and duties relate to the estates of deceased persons, to see that they go to the persons entitled to them.

---

* They derive their name from this circumstance: Each court has its district, including several counties, and as the law usually requires, for the convenience of suitors, that the court be held once or twice a year in each county, the judges travel from one county to another.

In some of the States of New England this system of courts does not exist. The highest court performs their duties, having both original and appellate jurisdiction. It will be noticed that New England is different from the rest of the country in many of her political institutions.

They take proof of wills and empower executors to act.* Where a person dies without a will the probate court appoints an *administrator*, who distributes the personal property (for distinction between personal and real property, see page 61) among the relatives to whom it belongs by law.† It has power to remove the executor or administrator if he does not do his duty; to settle his accounts; and decide disputes which arise, as to the distribution of the estate. Probate courts also take charge of the estates of minors whose parents have died, and appoint guardians for them. For this reason they are sometimes called *orphans' courts*. Appeals may be taken from these courts to the Supreme Court, or sometimes to the Circuit Courts.

8. Courts of Chancery exist in several States. They have power to grant certain kinds of relief that, in the States where they exist, the other courts can not; such as compelling a man to perform a contract, instead of awarding money as damages for his not doing it, or granting an injunction against one's doing an unlawful act. These are also called *courts of equity*. It is unnecessary to enumerate their powers, as in most States they do not exist, and there the other courts have all their powers.

9. Other Courts.—In some States there are other courts with various powers. *County courts*, or *courts of common pleas*, exist in some, having jurisdiction in civil cases, somewhat higher than justices' courts; *courts of sessions*

---

* A will is a writing by which a person directs to whom his property shall be given after his death. The Latin *probatus* means proof, from which the courts derive their name. An *executor* is a person appointed in a will to carry out its provisions.

† An administrator has no jurisdiction over the land owned by the deceased. That the heirs can take possession of without any authority from the court. An executor, in general, executes the will both as regards personal and real property.

and *courts of oyer and terminer,* where they exist, are courts of criminal jurisdiction; *police courts* are often established in cities with jurisdiction to try the lower criminal offences; large cities generally have additional courts.

10. Elections and Terms.—Judges are sometimes elected by the people, sometimes by the legislature, and sometimes appointed by the governor. The terms of office vary, being generally six to ten years in the higher courts, while justices of the peace are elected or appointed every one or two years. In a few States (in New England) the judges of the highest court hold office for life, or until seventy years of age. Like legislative and executive officers, they receive salaries fixed by law.

CHAPTER XX.

LEGAL PROCEEDINGS.

a. Impeachment.

1. Impeachment.—A complaint against the officer having been brought formally before the lower house of the legislature, it votes whether he shall be impeached or not, and if it is decided that there are sufficient grounds for the charge, *articles of impeachment* are prepared and delivered to the upper house, and a committee of *managers* is selected from the members of the lower house to conduct the prosecution.

2. Trial.—The upper house (senate) then convenes as a court, the accused person is summoned to answer the charge, and a time is fixed for the trial. The trial is conducted in much the same way as a trial in other courts, and at the close the senate votes upon his guilt, a two-thirds vote being generally required to convict. If convicted, the court may remove him from office, or disqualify him to hold any office in the State, for a time, or for life; or may both remove and disqualify him. This court can pronounce no other sentence. But if the act committed is a crime, the offender may also be indicted, tried, and punished in a court of justice.

b. *Proceedings in Ordinary Civil Cases.*

3. Parties.—In both civil and criminal cases the party suing is called the *plaintiff* (i.e. the one complaining), and the party sued the *defendant* (i.e. the one defending himself).*

We will now give a sketch of the ordinary steps in a civil action in their order.

4. Summons.—Except in the lowest courts, all the proceedings in a lawsuit are taken by means of written papers. This is that they may be preserved. The first paper is ordinarily a *summons*. This is a writ issued by the court at the instance of the plaintiff, and served upon the defendant, summoning him to appear in court. Generally this appearance is made not by coming into court in person,

---

* In a criminal case the State is the plaintiff, and the accused the defendant. The State, i.e. the whole people, are the ones injured by a crime. For example, in New York State the title of a criminal case is "The People of the State of New York against John Smith." Also, the person against whom the offence is committed has his civil remedy, a suit for damages, against the offender. So that in the case of a criminal offence (for instance, assault and battery) the injured party can sue the offender for damages, and the State can punish him at the same time.

but by the defendant's attorney* filing a notice in the clerk's office. If he does not appear within a certain time, the plaintiff may take judgment and issue execution immediately. (See page 83.)

5. Pleadings.—If the defendant appears, the plaintiff is then required to file or serve his *declaration* or *complaint*, setting forth what he claims, and the facts on which he bases the claim. The defendant then files or serves his *plea*, or *answer*, or *demurrer*,† setting forth his defence; that is, the reasons why he thinks he should not be compelled to do what the plaintiff demands. These papers are called the *pleadings*. Sometimes other papers are necessary. If the pleadings agree as to the facts, the matter is then presented to the court, and it makes its decision, without—what is popularly called—a trial. But if the pleadings do not agree as to the facts—if, for instance, the plea denies any fact the declaration sets out—this dispute must be settled by a trial.

6. Jury.—Trials may be had before the court alone, but in many cases either party may claim the right to have disputed facts decided by a *jury*.‡ In the higher courts a jury consists of twelve men; in justices' courts, of six. At every term of court (except in justices' courts) a number of men residing in the county are summoned to attend court to serve as jurors during the term, which lasts one or two weeks. From these the jury in each particular case is chosen by lot.

---

* In this connection an *attorney*, or *counsel*, is a lawyer who conducts a lawsuit for a person. In a broader sense, attorney often means an agent to transact any business.

† These words have different meanings, unnecessary to state here.

‡ So important is this right considered that it is guaranteed to every one, in certain cases, by most of the State constitutions. It was derived from England, where it has been enjoyed many centuries.

7. **Trial.**—As soon as the pleadings are filed or served either party may summon the other to trial. If either party does not appear at the trial, the other may have judgment against him. If the witnesses are unwilling to come, a subpœna (pronounced *suppēna*) may be issued to them. This is a writ from the court commanding them to attend, under heavy penalties if they do not. A judge always presides at the trial, and decides whether the evidence offered by either side is proper to be admitted in the case. The usual course of proceeding is as follows: the plaintiff's counsel opens the trial by briefly stating what the case is, and then examines such witnesses as he chooses, the defendant's counsel having the right to cross-examine each one, if he thinks the testimony needs to be made clearer; this examination and cross-examination is made by the counsel asking questions which the witness must answer, and the witness is not allowed to do anything but answer the questions put him; after the plaintiff has presented all his witnesses, the defendant's counsel, in turn, briefly states what his defence is, and examines his witnesses, the other side cross-examining each one if he desires; the defendant's counsel then makes an argument upon the case, and the plaintiff's counsel closes with his argument. This ends the trial if it is before the court alone. But if it is before a jury, the judge delivers a *charge* to the jury, giving them a summary of the evidence on both sides and pointing out to them the points they are to decide. The jury then retire, and deliberate in secret.

8. **Verdict.**—If the jury cannot agree, they are discharged, and another trial may be had; but if they agree, they return to court and announce their *verdict*. This word is from the Latin *verum*, true, and *dictum*, saying. In most States all the members of a jury must agree before a verdict can be rendered.

9. Judgment.—After a verdict, or decision of a case by the court, formal judgment is entered (i.e. filed or recorded), and the successful party may add as a part of it what are called *costs*. These are certain sums of money allowed to him to compensate for his expenses. It is considered just that the one who is decided to be in the wrong should pay all the expense.

10. Appeal.—If the defeated party thinks justice has not been done, he may appeal to the next higher court. This court does not try the case over again, but simply examines all that was done in the lower court to see if any error was committed. If there was none, it *affirms* the judgment; but if any—even a slight—error was committed, it *reverses* the judgment and grants a *new trial*, which is conducted in the same way as the first. In many cases, if either party is dissatisfied with the decision of the higher court he may appeal to a still higher one, which, in turn, affirms or reverses. In this way a single case may have three or four trials, and five or six appeals, though that is very unusual. Small cases cannot generally be appealed to the highest court.

11. Execution against Property.—After judgment is obtained against one, if he does not pay it, a writ called an *execution against the property* may be issued to the sheriff. This commands him to seize the debtor's property and sell it until he has sold enough to satisfy (i.e. pay) the judgment. Certain articles, such as household goods and clothing, cannot be sold by the sheriff.

12. Execution against the Person.—Formerly, in addition to the execution against property, an *execution against the person* could be issued in all cases. This commanded the sheriff to put the debtor in jail until he paid the judgment. But now this extreme remedy is abolished, except in cases where the judgment is obtained for some act implying moral turpitude, such as libel, assault, fraud, etc. In cases of ordinary debt, such as for goods sold, money borrowed, etc., this execution cannot be had.

c. Proceedings in Criminal Cases.

13. Indictment.*—It is usual for state constitutions to contain provisions requiring that before one can be tried for a criminal offence (except a petty one) he must be indicted by a grand jury. A *grand jury* is a body of citizens (usually twenty-three) summoned in every county several times during the year, to inquire what crimes have been committed in the county. An *indictment* is a formal accusation made by a grand jury against a person that he has committed a crime. The process of indictment is as follows: Some one, usually the district attorney, brings the fact of a crime to their notice; the jury then summon the witnesses † named and examine them; if twelve of the jurors vote that there is sufficient cause for putting him on trial, the indictment is drawn up by the district attorney, endorsed "a true bill" by the foreman of the grand jury, and then sent to the court. These proceedings are kept secret, in order to prevent the offender's escape.

14. Arrest and Bail.—A warrant may then be issued for the arrest of the accused. If arrested, he may give *bail*, except in cases of crimes punishable by death, like murder. Giving bail consists of giving a bond, by which the bondsmen agree to pay the State a certain sum of money if the prisoner does not appear when he is wanted. The prisoner is then released until his trial. He is then supposed to be

---

* Pronounced *inditement.*

† No witnesses in favor of the accused are examined by the grand jury.

in the custody of his bondsmen, and they can arrest him at any time.

15. Examination.—But often it is feared that if an indictment is awaited the offender may escape. In such case a complaint is sworn to before a justice of the peace, or other magistrate, and he issues a warrant. When the arrest is made the accused is brought before him, and he makes a short examination of the case. If the evidence is such that he thinks the accused should be tried, he commits him to prison to await the action of the grand jury, or if the case be not indictable, to be tried at the next court. He may then give bail.

16. Habeas Corpus.*—If the prisoner thinks that his arrest is unlawful, he, or any one in his interest, may apply to any judge of a higher court for a writ of *habeas corpus.* This commands the sheriff, or whoever has him in custody, to bring him before the judge. The case is not tried then, but the judge simply examines the case to see whether the arrest is lawful; that is, whether any crime is charged, or whether there is any proper complaint. If he decides that the prisoner is lawfully held, he remands him to prison; if not, he orders him released.

17. Trial.—Due notice being given to the prisoner, and a counsel to conduct his case being furnished him by the State, if he has none, he is brought to trial, and, except in

---

* This is the most famous writ in the law. It applies to all cases where one person is unlawfully restrained by another, as well as to persons charged with criminal offences. It is often used by a father to gain possession of his child which has been unlawfully taken from him. So important is it considered that state constitutions often provide that the right of having the writ shall not be suspended by the legislature except in time of rebellion or invasion. It protects the right of personal liberty by causing the ground of arrest or restraint to be examined by a competent judge.

petty cases, has the constitutional right to be tried by a jury. He is first called upon to *plead* to the indictment (i.e. answer it), and he may plead "guilty" or "not guilty." This is called *arraignment*. If he pleads "guilty," he is immediately sentenced; if "not guilty," the trial proceeds. The course of the trial is the same as in civil cases: the opening addresses; examination and cross-examination of the witnesses on each side; the arguments of counsel; the charge ; and the verdict (see page 82). After verdict he is discharged or sentenced, according as he is found innocent or guilty.

d. *Other Proceedings.*

18. In Probate Courts.—Here the proceedings, though somewhat different, bear a resemblance to those in other courts. Generally there is no contest; but when there is the court proceeds in much the same way as other courts, but without a jury.

19. Special Proceedings.—The proceedings already described do not embrace all the varieties. Courts are applied to for a great many objects, which cannot be enumerated here, and the proceedings taken differ in different classes of cases. But in all legal proceedings the object is to bring all the parties interested before the court, so that it may learn what all claim, and give each one a chance to disprove misstatements made by any one else.

REVIEW QUESTIONS.

General Principles of Government.

Necessity for Society and Government.

1. Why is civil society necessary to mankind?
2. From what does the right of private property come?
3. What is law? Why necessary?
4. Why is government necessary?

Classification of Rights and Law.

5. What is a right?
6. What are political rights? In what act does a man exercise them?
7. Name the different classes of civil rights.
8. To what class do religious rights belong?
9. What is the difference between the moral law and the law of nature?
10. What is the difference between the moral law and municipal law? Which is the broader? Why?

Forms of Government.

11. Name and define the three fundamental forms of government.
12. What is a despotism?
13. To what form of government does England belong? Is it absolute or limited?
14. Explain the difference between a Republic and a Pure Democracy.
15. To which form does the United States Government belong? To which do the State Governments? Why?

STATE GOVERNMENTS.

Constitution : Election : Departments.

1. What is a constitution in this country? How many are there here now?
2. How are constitutions framed? By whom, and how, adopted?
3. Name the usual qualifications of voters, as to age, sex, residence, property, character, and color.
4. Describe the manner of conducting an election.
5. What is registration?
6. What is the difference between a majority and a plurality? Which, usually, is necessary to elect a person?
7. How many departments of government are there? Give the name and duties of each. Why are they kept distinct?

Legislative Department.

8. Name the two branches of the legislature. Which is the larger house? Which the more select?
9. Are legislators elected or appointed?
10. How often do legislatures meet? What does organization consist of?
11. What is a quorum? How many usually constitute it (i.e. what proportion)?
12. Are the proceedings of legislatures open or secret?
13. Describe the usual method of enacting laws.
14. What are the purpose and use of committees?
15. What is a veto? Its effect?
16. Is a law valid which is passed with all the formalities which the constitution prescribes, but not according to the rules of the legislature?

Executive Department.

17. Who is the chief executive officer of a State? How does he differ from a king?
18. Name his principal powers.
19. Name the other high executive state officers, and their duties.
20. What are the territorial divisions of a State? Their purpose?
21. Which is the more important political division (county or town) in the Southern States? In New England?
22. What is a municipal corporation? Give some examples.
23. Name the principal county officers, and their duties.
24. Which represent the county, and which the State?
25. Name the principal town officers, and their duties.
26. Are officers of the executive department elected or appointed?
27. What is a city? A village? Why are they incorporated?

28. Are inhabitants of cities and villages subject to the general laws of the State?
29. In what particulars do municipal corporations differ from private? The State from other municipal corporations?
30. What is a tax? Its purpose?
31. Upon what kind of property are most of the taxes collected?
32. What are assessors?
33. How is a tax collected when the party will not pay it, in case he is taxed for personal property? How, in case he is taxed for land?
34. Explain why any government should furnish some education to its citizens? Why should we in this country especially?
35. How are common schools supported?
36. Name some public institutions supported by the State.
37. How does a railroad or canal company acquire its land?
38. Explain the difference between militia and a standing army.
39. Of what is a state militia composed? Of what the United States militia?
40. Who is the highest officer of the state militia?
41. What are volunteer regiments?

Judicial Department.

42. What duties does the judicial department perform?
43. What is impeachment? What body tries impeachments? What judgment may it render?
44. What is the difference between a civil and a criminal case? Between original and appellate jurisdiction?
45. Name the three grades of law courts in a State, with the usual jurisdiction of each. About how many courts are there in each grade?
46. What are the duties of probate courts?
47. Describe the progress of an ordinary civil case. Describe the course of a trial.
48. In what civil cases may a defendant be arrested?
49. What is an indictment? A grand jury?
50. Describe the progress of an ordinary criminal case.
51. Who is the plaintiff in a criminal case?

DIVISION III.

NATIONAL GOVERNMENT.

SECTION I.

ITS ORIGIN AND NATURE.

CHAPTER XXI.

GOVERNMENT BEFORE THE REVOLUTION.

1. The United States a Nation.—Besides the state governments that we have described, there is in this country another government, to which all the people of all the States are subject, and which, in its own sphere, has paramount authority over all the state governments. This is the United States Government. The people of all the states have, as a Nation, collectively adopted another constitution, the United States Constitution. This establishes another and superior government for all the people, which is therefore called the National Government. In this document the Nation is called "The United States of America." To assist the reader in understanding the Constitution and government of the United States, we shall first give a sketch of the governments which preceded the Revolution, and of the principal causes which led to it.

2. The Colonies.—Most of those who study this work probably know that our present state and national governments v this country. The first inhabitants (except the Indians) were *colonists*. A *colony* is a settlement of persons in a distant place or country, who remain subject to the government of the country from which they came. At the time of the Revolution there existed here thirteen Colonies, settled mostly from Great Britain, all subject to the British sovereign, but independent of each other.

3. Colonial Governments.—The political rights and privileges enjoyed by the Colonists as British subjects were limited. The people had not then, as now, constitutions of their own choice. There were colonial governments; but they were such as the king was pleased to establish, and, generally, might be changed at his pleasure. These governments were in *form* somewhat similar to that of our state governments. There was what might be called a legislature; also an executive or governor; and there were judges. But of the officers of these departments of the government, only the members of the lower branch of the legislature were elected by the people. The other branch was composed of a small number of men, called a *council;* but they were appointed by the king and subject to his control, as was also the governor, who had the power of an absolute negative or veto to any proposed law. And laws, after having received the assent of the governor, had to be sent to England and approved by the king before they could go into effect. The judges were appointed by the governor. The Colonies were also subject to the laws of the English Parliament.

4. Good Laws Denied.—Hence we see that the Colonists had no security for the passage of such laws as they wanted. And the consequence was that they were often denied good laws.

5. Oppressive Laws of Parliament.—Not only so; many laws enacted by Parliament were very unjust and oppressive.

The object of these laws was to secure to Great Britain alone the trade of the Colonies. One law declared that no goods should be imported by the Colonists but in English vessels; if brought in other vessels, both the goods and vessels were to be forfeited to the British Government. Another law declared that no iron wares should be manufactured by the Colonists, so as to compel them to buy of England. So also the Colonists were permitted to ship to foreign markets such products only as English merchants did not want. They were prohibited from selling abroad any wool, yarn, or woollen manufactured goods, in order to keep the foreign markets open for British wool and manufactures.

6. Duties.—One way taken to compel the Colonies to buy of England alone was to impose heavy duties on goods imported from anywhere else. For instance: The Colonists traded with the West India islands, some of which belonged to Great Britain, some to France, and some to Spain. To secure the whole trade to the British islands, the British Government imposed high duties upon the molasses, sugar, and other articles imported into the Colonies from the French and Spanish islands. The people of the Colonies were therefore obliged to import the above-mentioned goods from the British islands only, while, if there had been no duty, they could have obtained them more cheaply from the others.

7. Taxation without Representation.—Not satisfied with these acts, Parliament claimed the right to tax the Colonies "in all cases whatsoever;" and an act was passed accordingly, laying duties upon all tea, glass, paper, etc., imported into the Colonies; and the money thus collected was put into the British treasury. The Colonists petitioned the king and Parliament to repeal these obnoxious laws, claiming that under a free government there should be no *taxation without representation;* that is, that no legislative body had the right to tax them, unless they had representatives of their own in that body; and they had none in Parliament. These petitions were, however, disregarded.

8. Result.—The Colonies resisted the payment of these unjust taxes. Troops were then sent to compel submission, and the Colonists, too, began to arm. Finally, the Congress, which was a body of delegates from the several Colonies, giving up all hope of relief, declared by the Declaration of Independence, on July 4th, 1776, the Colonies to be free and independent States, no longer subject to the government of Great Britain. This declaration was maintained by a war which lasted about seven years, when Great Britain gave up the contest and acknowledged the independence of the States; and the *Revolution* was accomplished. By this declaration the thirteen Colonies became thirteen States, independent not only of Great Britain, but also, in most respects, of each other.

CHAPTER XXII.

THE CONFEDERATION.

1. Continental Congress.—As early as the year 1774, the Colonies united in the plan of a congress, to be composed of delegates chosen in all the Colonies, for the purpose of consulting on the common good and of adopting measures of resistance to the claims of the British Government. The Continental Congress, convened in May, 1775, conducted the affairs of the country until near the close of the war. This body was in reality a revolutionary body. It had nothing to define or limit its powers. But the people relied upon the honor, wisdom, and patriotism of its members, and acquiesced in their acts.

2. Confederation.—But it was seen from the first that the Colonies (now States, by the Declaration of Independence) ought to be united, and that a central government with clearly defined powers must be established. With a view to a permanent union the Congress, in November 1777, agreed upon a frame of government, contained in certain articles, called "Articles of Confederation and Perpetual Union between the States." These articles were to go into effect when they should have received the assent of all the States. But as the consent of the last State (Maryland) was not obtained until March, 1781, they went into operation only about two years before the close of the war.

3. Defective.—As a plan of national government, the Confederation was soon found to be very defective. The union formed under it was a very imperfect one. Having been framed in time of war, it had respect to the operations of war rather than to a state of peace. Its defects appeared almost as soon as it went into effect; and after the return of peace it was found that the union, instead of being strengthened and perpetuated by it, could be preserved only by a radical change.

4. Weakness.—The leading defect of the Confederation was its weakness. It consisted merely of a legislature, called the *Congress*, and had no executive or judicial departments. This body could do little more than recommend measures. As it could not legislate directly upon persons, its measures were to be carried into effect by the States; but the States were not in all cases willing, and some of them did at times refuse to do so, and Congress could not compel them. It belonged to Congress to determine the number of troops and the sums of money necessary to carry on the war, and to call on each State to raise its share; but Congress could not enforce its demands. It borrowed money in its own name, but it had no means of raising money to pay it. Hence we see that Congress was dependent for everything upon the good-will of thirteen independent States. It is a wonder that a government of such inherent weakness should bring the war to a successful issue. It was a sense of danger from abroad, rather than any power in the government, that induced a sufficient compliance with the ordinances of Congress to achieve the independence of the States.

5. Taxes and Duties.—Congress had no power to levy taxes or to impose duties. These powers were reserved to the States. Even during the war the necessary means to carry it on were with difficulty collected from the States. But after the war not only was money needed for the ordinary expenses of the government, but there was a heavy debt to be paid. Duties were necessary also to regulate foreign trade, but each State imposed such as it saw fit, and there was no uniformity. Hence American commerce was fast being destroyed through the want of power in the central government to regulate it.

6. Discord between States.—Another of the numerous troubles which arose from this imperfect union was the want of peace and harmony between the States. Laws were enacted in some States with a view to their own interests, which operated injuriously upon other States. This induced the latter to retaliate, by passing laws partial to themselves and injurious to the former. The States soon became disaffected toward each other; and their mutual jealousies and rivalries and animosities at length became so great as to cause fears that some of the States would become involved in war among themselves, and that thus the union would be broken up.

7. Attempts at Amendment.—In view of these difficulties, attempts were made to change the Articles of Confederation so as to give the Congress more power, especially in the matter of regulating trade; but the attempts failed.

8. Convention of 1786.—In January 1786 the legislature of Virginia proposed a convention of commissioners from all the States, to take into consideration the situation and trade of the United States and the necessity of a uniform system of commercial regulations. A meeting was accordingly held at Annapolis in September 1786; but as commissioners from only five States * attended, the commissioners deemed it unadvisable to proceed to business relating to an object in which all the States were concerned; but they united in a report to the several States and to Congress, in which they recommended the calling of a general convention of delegates from all the States, to meet in Philadelphia in May 1787, with a view not only to the regulation of commerce, but to such other amendments of the Articles of Confederation as were necessary to render them "adequate to the exigencies of the union."

9. Convention of 1787.—In pursuance of this recommendation, Congress, in February 1787, passed a resolution providing for a convention. All the States except Rhode Island appointed delegates, who met pursuant to appointment and framed the present Constitution of the United States. They also recommended it to be laid by Congress before the several States, to be by them considered and ratified in conventions of representatives of the people.

10. Adoption of Constitution.—By this Constitution, as

---

* New York, New Jersey, Pennsylvania, Delaware, and Virginia.

soon as the people of nine States ratified it, it was to go into effect as to the States so ratifying. Conventions of the people were accordingly held in all the States. The ninth State, New Hampshire, sent its ratification to Congress in July 1788; and measures were taken by Congress to put the new government into operation. North Carolina and Rhode Island, the last States to accept the Constitution, did not send their ratifications until the year after the government was organized.

CHAPTER XXIII.

THE UNION UNDER THE CONSTITUTION.

1. Confederacy and Nation.—The Confederation and the Union under the Constitution were each a union of the States, but they differed vastly from each other. This difference may be best summed up by saying that the first make a Confederacy, the second a Nation.* Under the Confederation the States, though united as States "in a firm league of friendship with each other," yet expressly "retained each its sovereignty, freedom and independence."

---

* A *confederacy* is a league, or compact between individuals whether persons or nations: a nation, as distinguished from a confederacy, is a people indissolubly bound together as a unit, a single people. One is a combination, the other a consolidation. There is another sense in which the word nation is often used, that of a people, or combination of peoples, having a common central authority, which represents them in all relations with foreign nations. The States were never known or treated by foreign powers as separate nations, and therefore in this sense the whole people were one nation even under the Confederation. Further than this, it may be said that even before the Constitution the whole people, besides being bound together by ties of common parentage and mutual dependence, often acted as a consolidate

The people were citizens of the several States rather than of a consolidated nation. Under the Constitution the States are no longer sovereign. The Nation is above them, and they can do nothing contrary to the Constitution. They have in many respects surrendered their sovereignty to the Nation for the good of all. If they attempt to withdraw, the Nation can coerce them.* The people of the States are also citizens of the United States. We will give in the following sections the chief differences between the Confederation and the present Union, which taken together make one a Confederacy and the other a Nation.

2. Name.—The document which established the Confederation professed in its name to make nothing but a league between the States, as States, calling itself "Articles of Confederation . . . between the States." The Constitution, on the other hand, professes to make a union of the people, and not of the States: thus its preamble reads, "We, the People of the United States . . . do ordain and establish this Constitution."

3. By Whom Adopted.—The Articles of Confederation were adopted by the state legislatures, acting for the States, as States; the Constitution was adopted by conventions elected by the people in the several States. By whom they were framed is of little import.

4. Power.—But the chief difference between the two was in their power. We have seen that the Confederation had no power except to pass laws, and States and individuals could disobey them without fear of punishment, for

---

* At the time of the late Civil War the Southern States claimed that the Nation was but a Confederation, and that therefore they could withdraw. This they attempted to do, and set up a government of their own, calling it the "Confederate States of America." But—if force of arms can ever settle a logical question—it is now settled that our country is not a mere confederation, but a Nation.

it had no executive department to enforce, and no judicial department to judge of, its laws. But the Constitution gives the National Government all necessary powers to enforce obedience to its laws; a complete executive department, with armies and money (or the power to raise them) at its command; and also a judicial department free from state control.

5. State Equality.—Again, under the Confederation, as in confederacies generally, the States were equal. They were entitled to an equal number of delegates in the Congress, in which they voted by States, each State having one vote; that is, if a majority of the delegates of a State voted in favor of or against a proposed measure, the vote of the State was so counted; and a proposition having in its favor a majority of the States was carried. Under the Constitution both branches of the legislature vote *per capita*, the vote of each member counting one, and in the lower branch the representation is according to population, and thus the larger States have more members. The President, too, is elected, not by States, but by a majority vote of the Electors. (See pages 126, 162.)

6. National Government.—The government of the Confederation, although sometimes called the National Government, was not really such, nor was it generally so regarded, as appears from the proceedings of the Convention that framed the Constitution. Early in the session of the Convention a resolution was offered, declaring "That a National Government ought to be established, consisting of a supreme legislative, judiciary, and executive." This resolution was strongly opposed by a large portion of the delegates, because it proposed to establish a *national* government.' They were in favor of continuing the Confederation with a slight enlargement of the powers of Congress, so as to give that body the power to lay and collect taxes and to regulate commerce. But the friends of a national government prevailed; and history has proved their wisdom.

7. Federal Union.—But although the present government, with its three departments, its powers, and its supremacy over the States, is properly a national government, yet it is not wholly such, but partly national and partly federal; some of the federal features of the Confederation having been retained in the Constitution, as will appear on a further examination of this instrument. Hence the Union is still called, with propriety, the *Federal Union*, and the government the *Federal Government*.

CHAPTER XXIV.

CONSTITUTION OF THE UNITED STATES.

[NOTE.—The following is the text of the Constitution and Amendments. It should be studied until the pupil can give the subject and substance of each paragraph. The titles of the articles and sections form no part of the document, but are added here for the purpose of convenience in reference. The large numbers at the left are placed there that the paragraphs may be referred to by number in the rest of the book.]

PREAMBLE.

1 WE, the People of the United States, in order to form a more perfect union, establish justice, insure domestic tranquillity, provide for the common defence, promote the general welfare, and secure the blessings of liberty to ourselves and our posterity, do ordain and establish this Constitution for the United States of America.

ARTICLE I.

Legislative Department.

Section 1.—Division into Two Houses.

1. All legislative powers herein granted shall be vested in a Congress of the United States, which shall consist of a Senate and House of Representatives.

Section 2.—House of Representatives.

1. The House of Representatives shall be composed of members chosen every second year by the people of the several States; and the electors in each State shall have the qualifications requisite for electors of the most numerous branch of the State Legislature.

2. No person shall be a Representative who shall not have attained to the age of twenty-five years, and been seven years a citizen of the United States, and who shall not, when elected, be an inhabitant of that State in which he shall be chosen.

3. Representatives and direct taxes shall be apportioned among the several States which may be included within this Union, according to their respective numbers, which shall be determined by adding to the whole number of free persons, including those bound to service for a term of years, and excluding Indians not taxed, three fifths of all other persons. The actual enumeration shall be made within three years after the first meeting of the Congress of the United States, and within every subsequent term of ten years, in such manner as they shall by law direct. The number of Representatives shall not exceed one for every thirty thousand, but each State shall have at least one Representative; and until such enumeration shall be made, the State of New Hampshire shall be entitled to choose *three;* Massachusetts, *eight;* Rhode Island and Providence Plantations, *one;* Connecticut, *five;* New York, *six;* New Jersey, *four;* Pennsylvania, *eight;* Delaware, *one;* Mary-

land, *six;* Virginia, *ten;* North Carolina, *five;* South Carolina, *five;* and Georgia, *three.*

4. When vacancies happen in the representation from any State, the executive authority thereof shall issue writs of election to fill such vacancies.

5. The House of Representatives shall choose their Speaker and other officers, and shall have the sole power of impeachment.

SECTION 3.—Senate.

1. The Senate of the United States shall be composed of two Senators from each State, chosen by the Legislature thereof, for six years; and each Senator shall have one vote.

2. Immediately after they shall be assembled in consequence of the first election, they shall be divided, as equally as may be, into three classes. The seats of the Senators of the first class shall be vacated at the expiration of the second year; of the second class at the expiration of the fourth year; and of the third class at the expiration of the sixth year; so that one third may be chosen every second year; and if vacancies happen, by resignation or otherwise, during the recess of the Legislature of any State, the Executive thereof may make temporary appointments, until the next meeting of the Legislature, which shall then fill such vacancies.

3. No person shall be a Senator who shall not have attained to the age of thirty years, and been nine years a citizen of the United States, and who shall not, when elected, be an inhabitant of that State for which he shall be chosen

4. The Vice-President of the United States shall be President of the Senate, but shall have no vote, unless they be equally divided.

5. The Senate shall choose their other officers and also a President *pro tempore*, in the absence of the Vice-President, or when he shall exercise the office of President of the United States

6. The Senate shall have the sole power to try all impeachments: when sitting for that purpose, they shall be

States is tried, the Chief-Justice shall preside; and no person shall be convicted without the concurrence of two-thirds of the members present.

14. 7. Judgment, in cases of impeachment, shall not extend further than to removal from office, and disqualification to hold and enjoy any office of honor, trust, or profit, under the United States; but the party convicted shall, nevertheless, be liable and subject to indictment, trial, judgment and punishment, according to law.

SECTION 4.—Elections and Meetings of Congress.

15. 1. The times, places, and manner of holding elections for Senators and Representatives shall be prescribed in each State by the Legislature thereof; but the Congress may at any time, by law, make or alter such regulations, except as to the places of choosing Senators.

16. 2. The Congress shall assemble at least once in every year; and such meeting shall be on the first Monday in December, unless they shall, by law, appoint a different day.

SECTION 5.—Powers and Duties of the Houses.

17. 1. Each House shall be the judge of the elections, returns, and qualifications of its own members; and a majority of each shall constitute a quorum to do business; but a smaller number may adjourn from day to day, and may be authorized to compel the attendance of absent members, in such manner, and under such penalties, as each House may provide.

18. 2. Each House may determine the rules of its proceedings, punish its members for disorderly behavior, and, with the concurrence of two-thirds, expel a member.

19. 3. Each House shall keep a journal of its proceedings, and from time to time publish the same, excepting such parts as may, in their judgment, require secrecy; and the yeas and nays of the members of either House, on any question, shall, at the desire of one-fifth of those present, be entered on the journal.

20. 4. Neither House, during the session of Congress, shall, without the consent of the other, adjourn for more than

three days, nor to any other place than that in which the two Houses shall be sitting.

SECTION 6.—Privileges of and Prohibitions upon Members.

21 1 The Senators and Representatives shall receive a compensation for their services, to be ascertained by law, and paid out of the treasury of the United States. They shall, in all cases except treason, felony, and breach of the peace, be privileged from arrest during their attendance at the session of their respective Houses, and in going to and returning from the same, and for any speech or debate in either House, they shall not be questioned in any other place.

22 2. No Senator or Representative shall, during the time for which he was elected, be appointed to any civil office under the authority of the United States, which shall have been created, or the emoluments whereof shall have been increased, during such time; and no person holding any office under the United States shall be a member of either House during his continuance in office.

SECTION 7.—Revenue Bills: President's Veto.

23 1. All bills for raising revenue shall originate in the House of Representatives; but the Senate may propose, or concur with, amendments, as on other bills.

24 2. Every bill which shall have passed the House of Representatives and the Senate shall, before it become a law, be presented to the President of the United States; if he approve, he shall sign it; but if not, he shall return it, with his objections, to that House in which it shall have originated, who shall enter the objections at large on their journal, and proceed to reconsider it. If, after such reconsideration, two-thirds of that House shall agree to pass the bill, it shall be sent, together with the objections, to the other House, by which it shall likewise be reconsidered, and, if approved by two thirds of that House, it shall become a law But, in all such cases, the votes of both Houses shall be determined by yeas and nays, and the names of the persons voting for and against the bill shall be entered on the journal of each House respectively. If any bill shall not be returned by the President within ten days (Sundays excepted) after it shall have been presented to him, the same shall be a law, in like manner as if he had signed it, unless the Congress, by their adjournment, prevent its return, in which case it shall not be a law.

25. 3. Every order, resolution, or vote to which the concurrence of the Senate and House of Representatives may be necessary (except on a question of adjournment), shall be presented to the President of the United States, and before the same shall take effect shall be approved by him, or, being disapproved by him, shall be repassed by two-thirds of the Senate and House of Representatives, according to the rules and limitations prescribed in the case of a bill.

Section 8.—Legislative Powers of Congress.

The Congress shall have power:

26. 1. To lay and collect taxes, duties, imposts, and excises to pay the debts and provide for the common defence and general welfare of the United States; but all duties, imposts, and excises shall be uniform throughout the United States:

27. 2. To borrow money on the credit of the United States:

28. 3. To regulate commerce with foreign nations, and among the several States, and with the Indian tribes:

29. 4. To establish a uniform rule of naturalization, and uniform laws on the subject of bankruptcies throughout the United States:

30. 5. To coin money; to regulate the value thereof, and of foreign coin; and fix the standard of weights and measures.

31. 6. To provide for the punishment of counterfeiting the securities and current coin of the United States:

32. 7. To establish post-offices and post-roads:

33. 8. To promote the progress of science and useful arts, by securing for limited times, to authors and inventors, the exclusive right to their respective writings and discoveries:

34. 9. To constitute tribunals inferior to the Supreme Court.

35. 10. To define and punish piracies and felonies committed on the high seas, and offences against the law of nations:

36. 11. To declare war; grant letters of marque and reprisal; and make rules concerning captures on land and water:

37. 12. To raise and support armies; but no appropriation of money to that use shall be for a longer term than two years:

38. 13. To provide and maintain a navy:

39. 14. To make rules for the government and regulation of the land and naval forces:

40. 15. To provide for calling forth the militia to execute the laws of the Union, suppress insurrections, and repel invasions:

41. 16. To provide for organizing, arming, and disciplining the militia, and for governing such part of them as may be employed in the service of the United States; reserving to the States respectively the appointment of the officers, and the authority of training the militia according to the discipline prescribed by Congress:

42. 17. To exercise exclusive legislation in all cases whatsoever over such district (not exceeding ten miles square) as may, by cession of particular States and the acceptance of Congress, become the seat of the government of the United States, and to exercise like authority over all places purchased by the consent of the Legislature of the State in which the same shall be, for the erection of forts, magazines, arsenals, dock-yards, and other needful buildings: And

43. 18. To make all laws which shall be necessary and proper for carrying into execution the foregoing powers, and all other powers vested by this Constitution in the government of the United States, or in any department or officer thereof.

SECTION 9.—Prohibitions upon the United States.

44. 1. The migration or importation of such persons as any of the States now existing shall think proper to admit, shall not be prohibited by the Congress prior to the year one thousand eight hundred and eight; but a tax or duty may be imposed on such importation, not exceeding ten dollars for each person.

45. 2. The privilege of the writ of habeas corpus shall not be suspended unless when, in cases of rebellion or invasion,

46   3. No bill of attainder or ex post facto law shall be passed.

47   4. No capitation or other direct tax shall be laid, unless in proportion to the census or enumeration hereinbefore directed to be taken.

48   5. No tax or duty shall be laid on articles exported from any State. No preference shall be given, by any regulation of commerce or revenue, to the ports of one State over those of another; nor shall vessels bound to or from one State be obliged to enter, clear, or pay duties in another.

49   6. No money shall be drawn from the treasury, but in consequence of appropriations made by law; and a regular statement and account of the receipts and expenditures of all public money shall be published from time to time.

50   7. No title of nobility shall be granted by the United States; and no person holding any office of profit or trust under them shall, without the consent of the Congress, accept of any present, emolument, office, or title of any kind whatever, from any king, prince, or foreign State.

SECTION 10.—Prohibitions upon the States.

51   1. No State shall enter into any treaty, alliance, or confederation; grant letters of marque and reprisal; coin money; emit bills of credit; make anything but gold and silver coin a tender in payment of debts; pass any bill of attainder, ex post facto law, or law impairing the obligation of contracts; or grant any title of nobility.

52   2. No State shall, without the consent of the Congress, lay any imposts or duties on imports or exports, except what may be absolutely necessary for executing its inspection laws; and the net produce of all duties and imposts laid by any State on imports or exports, shall be for the use of the treasury of the United States; and all such laws shall be subject to the revision and control of the Congress. No State shall, without the consent of Congress, lay any duty of tonnage, keep troops or ships of war in time of peace, enter into any agreement or compact with another State, or with a foreign power, or engage in war unless actually invaded, or in such imminent danger as will not admit of delay.

ARTICLE II.

EXECUTIVE DEPARTMENT: THE PRESIDENT AND VICE-PRESIDENT.

SECTION 1.—Term: Election: Qualifications: Salary: Oath of Office.

53 1. The executive power shall be vested in a President of the United States of America. He shall hold his office during the term of four years, and, together with the Vice-President, chosen for the same term, be elected as follows:

54 2. Each State shall appoint, in such manner as the Legislature thereof may direct, a number of Electors equal to the whole number of Senators and Representatives to which the State may be entitled in the Congress; but no Senator or Representative, or person holding an office of trust or profit under the United States, shall be appointed an Elector.

The following clause has been superseded by Article XII. of the Amendments:

55 3. The Electors shall meet in their respective States, and vote by ballot for two persons, of whom one at least shall not be an inhabitant of the same State with themselves. And they shall make a list of all the persons voted for, and of the number of votes for each, which list they shall sign and certify, and transmit, sealed, to the seat of the government of the United States, directed to the President of the Senate. The President of the Senate shall, in the presence of the Senate and House of Representatives, open all the certificates, and the votes shall then be counted. The person having the greatest number of votes shall be the President, if such number be a majority of the whole number of Electors appointed, and if there be more than one who have such majority, and have an equal number of votes, then the House of Representatives shall immediately choose by ballot one of them for President; and if no person have a majority, then, from the five highest on the list, the said House shall, in like manner, choose the President. But in choosing the President, the votes shall be taken by States, the representation from each State having one vote; a quorum for this purpose shall consist of a member or members from two-thirds of the States, and a majority of the States shall be necessary to a choice. In every case, after the choice of the President, the person having the greatest number of votes of the Electors shall be the Vice-President. But if there should remain two or more who have equal votes, the Senate shall choose from them, by ballot, the Vice-President.

56 4. The Congress may determine the time of choosing the Electors, and the day on which they shall give their votes, which day shall be the same throughout the United States.

57 5. No person except a natural born citizen, or a citizen of the United States at the time of the adoption of this Constitution, shall be eligible to the office of President; neither shall any person be eligible to that office who shall not have attained to the age of thirty-five years, and been fourteen years a resident within the United States.

58 6. In case of the removal of the President from office, or of his death, resignation, or inability to discharge the powers and duties of the said office, the same shall devolve on the Vice-President, and the Congress may, by law, provide for the case of removal, death, resignation, or inability, both of the President and Vice President, declaring what officer shall then act as President; and such officer shall act accordingly, until the disability be removed, or a President shall be elected.

59 7. The President shall, at stated times, receive for his services a compensation, which shall neither be increased nor diminished during the period for which he shall have been elected; and he shall not receive, within that period, any other emolument from the United States, or any of them.

60 8. Before he enter on the execution of his office, he shall take the following oath or affirmation:

"I do solemnly swear (or affirm) that I will faithfully execute the office of President of the United States; and will, to the best of my ability, preserve, protect, and defend the Constitution of the United States."

SECTION 2.—President's Executive Powers.

61 1. The President shall be commander in chief of the army and navy of the United States, and of the militia of the several States when called into the actual service of the United States; he may require the opinion, in writing, of the principal officer in each of the executive Departments, upon any subject relating to the duties of their respective offices; and he shall have power to grant reprieves and

pardons for offences against the United States, except in cases of impeachment.

62. 2. He shall have power by and with the advice and consent of the Senate to make treaties, provided two-thirds of the Senators present concur; and he shall nominate, and by and with the advice and consent of the Senate shall appoint, ambassadors, other public ministers and consuls, judges of the Supreme Court, and all other officers of the United States whose appointments are not herein otherwise provided for, and which shall be established by law: but the Congress may, by law, vest the appointment of such inferior officers as they think proper, in the President alone, in the courts of law, or in the Heads of Departments.

63. 3. The President shall have power to fill up all vacancies that may happen during the recess of the Senate, by granting commissions which shall expire at the end of their next session.

SECTION 3.—President's Executive Powers (continued).

64. 1. He shall from time to time give to the Congress information of the state of the Union; and recommend to their consideration such measures as he shall judge necessary and expedient. He may, on extraordinary occasions, convene both Houses, or either of them; and in case of disagreement between them, with respect to the time of adjournment, he may adjourn them to such time as he shall think proper. He shall receive ambassadors and other public ministers. He shall take care that the laws be faithfully executed; and shall commission all the officers of the United States.

SECTION 4.—Impeachment.

65. 1. The President, Vice-President, and all civil officers of the United States shall be removed from office on impeachment for, and conviction of, treason, bribery, or other high crimes and misdemeanors.

ARTICLE III.

Judicial Department.

Section 1.—Courts: Terms of Office.

66 1. The judicial power of the United States shall be vested in one Supreme Court, and in such inferior Courts as the Congress may, from time to time, ordain and establish. The judges both of the Supreme and inferior Courts shall hold their offices during good behavior; and shall, at stated times, receive for their services a compensation which shall not be diminished during their continuance in office.

Section 2.—Jurisdiction.

67 1. The judicial power shall extend to all cases in law and equity arising under this Constitution, the laws of the United States and treaties made, or which shall be made, under their authority; to all cases affecting ambassadors, other public ministers, and consuls; to all cases of admiralty and maritime jurisdiction; to controversies to which the United States shall be a party, to controversies between two or more States; between a State and citizens of another State; between citizens of different States; between citizens of the same State claiming lands under grants of different States; and between a State, or the citizens thereof, and foreign States, citizens, or subjects.

68 2. In all cases affecting ambassadors, other public ministers and consuls, and those in which a State shall be a party, the Supreme Court shall have original jurisdiction. In all the other cases before mentioned, the Supreme Court shall have appellate jurisdiction, both as to law and fact, with such exceptions, and under such regulations, as the Congress shall make.

69 3. The trial of all crimes, except in cases of impeachment, shall be by jury; and such trial shall be held in the State where the said crimes shall have been committed; but when not committed within any State, the trial shall be at

such place or places as the Congress may by law have directed.

SECTION 3.—Treason.

70 1. Treason against the United States shall consist only in levying war against them, or in adhering to their enemies, giving them aid and comfort. No person shall be convicted of treason, unless on the testimony of two witnesses to the same overt act, or on confession in open court.

71 2. The Congress shall have power to declare the punishment of treason; but no attainder of treason shall work corruption of blood, or forfeiture, except during the life of the person attainted.

ARTICLE IV.

RELATIONS OF STATES.

SECTION 1.—Public Records.

72 1. Full faith and credit shall be given, in each State, to the public acts, records, and judicial proceedings of every other State. And the Congress may, by general laws, prescribe the manner in which such acts, records, and proceedings shall be proved, and the effect thereof.

SECTION 2.—Rights in one State of Citizens of another.

73 1. The citizens of each State shall be entitled to all the privileges and immunities of citizens in the several States.

74 2. A person charged in any State with treason, felony, or other crime, who shall flee from justice and be found in another State, shall, on demand of the executive authority of the State from which he fled, be delivered up, to be removed to the State having jurisdiction of the crime.

75 3. No person held to service or labor in one State, under the laws thereof, escaping into another, shall, in consequence of any law or regulation therein, be discharged from such service or labor; but shall be delivered up on claim of the party to whom such service or labor may be due.

Section 3.—New States: Territories.

76 1. New States may be admitted by the Congress into this Union; but no new State shall be formed or erected within the jurisdiction of any other State, nor any State be formed by the junction of two or more States, or parts of States, without the consent of the Legislatures of the States concerned, as well as of the Congress.

77 2. The Congress shall have power to dispose of, and make all needful rules and regulations respecting, the territory or other property belonging to the United States; and nothing in this Constitution shall be so construed as to prejudice any claims of the United States, or of any particular State.

Section 4.—Protection afforded to States by the Nation.

78 1. The United States shall guarantee to every State in this Union a republican form of government; and shall protect each of them against invasion, and on application of the Legislature, or of the Executive (when the Legislature cannot be convened) against domestic violence.

ARTICLE V.

Amendment.

79 The Congress, whenever two-thirds of both Houses shall deem it necessary, shall propose amendments to this Constitution, or, on the application of the Legislatures of two-thirds of the several States, shall call a convention for proposing amendments; which, in either case, shall be valid to all intents and purposes, as part of this Constitution, when ratified by the Legislatures of three-fourths of the several States, or by conventions in three-fourths thereof, as the one or the other mode of ratification may be proposed by the Congress: provided, that no amendment which may be made prior to the year one thousand eight hundred and eight shall in any manner affect the first and fourth clauses

in the ninth section of the first article; and that no State without its consent, shall be deprived of its equal suffrage in the Senate.

ARTICLE VI.

NATIONAL DEBTS: SUPREMACY OF NATIONAL LAW: OATH.

80. **1.** All debts contracted, and engagements entered into, before the adoption of this Constitution shall be as valid against the United States under this Constitution as under the Confederation.

81. **2.** This Constitution, and the laws of the United States which shall be made in pursuance thereof, and all treaties made or which shall be made under the authority of the United States, shall be the supreme law of the land, and the judges in every State shall be bound thereby, anything in the Constitution or laws of any State to the contrary notwithstanding.

82. **3.** The Senators and Representatives before mentioned, and the members of the several Legislatures, and all executive and judicial officers, both of the United States and of the several States, shall be bound, by oath or affirmation, to support this Constitution; but no religious test shall ever be required as a qualification to any office or public trust under the United States.

ARTICLE VII.

ESTABLISHMENT OF CONSTITUTION.

83. The ratification of the conventions of nine States shall be sufficient for the establishment of this Constitution between the States so ratifying the same.

[Constitution ratified by States, 1787-1790.]

AMENDMENTS.

ARTICLE I.

Freedom of Religion, of Speech, and of the Press: Right of Petition.

84   Congress shall make no law respecting an establishment of religion, or prohibiting the free exercise thereof; or abridging the freedom of speech or of the press; or the right of the people peaceably to assemble, and to petition the government for a redress of grievances.

[Adopted 1791.]

ARTICLE II.

Right to Keep Arms.

85   A well-regulated militia being necessary to the security of a free State, the right of the people to keep and bear arms shall not be infringed.

[Adopted 1791.]

ARTICLE III.

Quartering of Soldiers in Private Houses.

86   No soldier shall, in time of peace, be quartered in any house without the consent of the owner; nor in a time of war, but in a manner to be prescribed by law.

[Adopted 1791.]

ARTICLE IV.

Search Warrants.

87   The right of the people to be secure in their persons, houses, papers, and effects, against unreasonable searches and seizures, shall not be violated; and no warrant shall

issue but upon probable cause, supported by oath or affirmation, and particularly describing the place to be searched and the person or things to be seized.
[Adopted 1791.]

ARTICLE V.

Criminal Proceedings.

88. No person shall be held to answer for a capital or otherwise infamous crime, unless on a presentment or indictment of a grand jury, except in cases arising in the land or naval forces, or in the militia when in actual service, in time of war or public danger; nor shall any person be subject, for the same offence, to be twice put in jeopardy of life or limb, nor shall be compelled, in any criminal case, to be a witness against himself; nor be deprived of life, liberty, or property without due process of law; nor shall private property be taken for public use without just compensation.
[Adopted 1791.]

ARTICLE VI.

Criminal Proceedings.

89. In all criminal prosecutions, the accused shall enjoy the right to a speedy and public trial by an impartial jury of the State and district wherein the crime shall have been committed, which district shall have been previously ascertained by law, and to be informed of the nature and cause of the accusation; to be confronted with the witnesses against him; to have compulsory process for obtaining witnesses in his favor; and to have the assistance of counsel for his defence.
[Adopted 1791.]

ARTICLE VII.

Jury Trial in Civil Cases.

90. In suits at common law, where the value in controversy shall exceed twenty dollars, the right of trial by jury shall

be preserved, and no fact tried by a jury shall be otherwise re-examined in any court of the United States than according to the rules of the common law.

[Adopted 1791.]

ARTICLE VIII.

Excessive Punishments.

91   Excessive bail shall not be required, nor excessive fines imposed, nor cruel and unusual punishments inflicted.

[Adopted 1791.]

ARTICLE IX.

Rights of People not named.

92   The enumeration in the Constitution of certain rights shall not be construed to deny or disparage others retained by the people.

[Adopted 1791.]

ARTICLE X.

Powers reserved to States.

93   The powers not delegated to the United States, by the Constitution, nor prohibited by it to the States, are reserved to the States respectively, or to the people.

[Adopted 1791.]

ARTICLE XI.

Suits against States.

94   The judicial power of the United States shall not be construed to extend to any suit in law or equity, commenced or prosecuted against one of the United States by citizens of another State, or by citizens or subjects of any foreign State.

[Adopted 1798.]

ARTICLE XII.

Election of President and Vice-President.

95   1. The Electors shall meet in their respective States and vote by ballot for President and Vice-President, one of whom at least shall not be an inhabitant of the same State with themselves; they shall name in their ballots the person voted for as President, and in distinct ballots the person voted for as Vice-President, and they shall make distinct lists of all persons voted for as President, and of all persons voted for as Vice-President, and of the number of votes for each, which lists they shall sign and certify, and transmit, sealed, to the seat of the government of the United States, directed to the President of the Senate;—the President of the Senate shall, in the presence of the Senate and House of Representatives, open all the certificates, and the votes shall then be counted;—the person having the greatest number of votes for President shall be the President, if such number be a majority of the whole number of Electors appointed; and if no person have such majority, then, from the persons having the highest numbers, not exceeding three, on the list of those voted for as President, the House of Representatives shall choose immediately, by ballot, the President. But in choosing the President, the votes shall be taken by States, the Representatives from each State having one vote; a quorum for this purpose shall consist of a member or members from two-thirds of the States, and a majority of all the States shall be necessary to a choice. And if the House of Representatives shall not choose a President whenever the right of choice shall devolve upon them, before the fourth day of March next following, then the Vice-President shall act as President, as in the case of the death or other constitutional disability of the President.

96   2. The person having the greatest number of votes as Vice-President shall be the Vice-President, if such number be a majority of the whole number of Electors appointed; and if no person have a majority, then, from the two high-

President; a quorum for the purpose shall consist of two-thirds of the whole number of Senators, and a majority of the whole number shall be necessary to a choice.

3. But no person constitutionally ineligible to the office of President shall be eligible to that of Vice-President of the United States.

[Adopted 1804.]

ARTICLE XIII.

Slavery.

Section 1. Abolition of Slavery.

Neither slavery nor involuntary servitude, except as a punishment for crime, whereof the party shall have been duly convicted, shall exist within the United States, or any place subject to their jurisdiction.

Section 2. Power of Congress.

Congress shall have power to enforce this article by appropriate legislation.

[Adopted 1865.]

ARTICLE XIV.

Civil Rights : Apportionment of Representatives : Political Disabilities : Public Debt.

Section 1. Civil Rights.

All persons born or naturalized in the United States, and subject to the jurisdiction thereof, are citizens of the United States and of the State wherein they reside. No State shall make or enforce any law which shall abridge the privileges or immunities of citizens of the United States; nor shall any State deprive any person of life, liberty, or property without due process of law, nor deny to any person within its jurisdiction the equal protection of the laws.

Section 2. Apportionment of Representatives.

100   Representatives shall be apportioned among the several States according to their respective numbers, counting the whole number of persons in each State, excluding Indians not taxed. But when the right to vote at any election for the choice of Electors for President and Vice-President of the United States, Representatives in Congress, the executive and judicial officers of a State, or the members of the Legislature thereof, is denied to any of the male inhabitants of such State, being twenty-one years of age, and citizens of the United States, or in any way abridged, except for participation in rebellion or other crime, the basis of representation therein shall be reduced in the proportion which the number of such male citizens shall bear to the whole number of male citizens twenty-one years of age in such State.

Section 3. Political Disabilities.

101   No person shall be a Senator or Representative in Congress, or Elector of President and Vice-President, or hold any office, civil or military, under the United States, or under any State, who, having previously taken an oath, as a member of Congress, or as an officer of the United States, or as a member of any State Legislature, or as an executive or judicial officer of any State, to support the Constitution of the United States, shall have engaged in insurrection or rebellion against the same, or given aid or comfort to the ememies thereof. But Congress may, by a vote of two-thirds of each House, remove such disability.

Section 4. Public Debt.

102   The validity of the public debt of the United States, authorized by law, including debts incurred for payment of pensions and bounties for services in suppressing insurrection or rebellion, shall not be questioned. But neither the United States nor any State shall assume or pay any debt or obligation incurred in aid of insurrection or rebellion against the United States, or any claim for

SUBJECT ANALYSIS.

I. Constitution.

THE NATIONAL GOVERNMENT.

- I. **Legislative Department**; [Art. I.]
  - I. Its Composition;
    - 1. Division into Two Houses, [Sec. 1.]
    - 2. House of Representatives, [Sec. 2.]
    - 3. Senate. [Sec. 3.]
  - II. Legislative Regulations;
    - 1. Elections and Meetings, [Sec. 4.]
    - 2. Powers and Duties, [Sec. 5.] (except law-making powers,)
    - 3. Privileges of and Prohibitions upon Members. [Sec. 6.]
  - III. President's Veto Power. [Sec. 7.]
  - IV. Legislative Powers of Congress. [Sec. 8.]
  - V. Prohibitions upon the United States. [Sec. 9.]
  - VI. Prohibitions upon the States.* [Sec. 10.]
- II. **Executive Department**—President and Vice-President; [Art. II.]
  - 1. (1) Term, (2) Election, (3) Qualifications, (4) Salary, (5) Oath, [Sec. 1.]
  - 2. President's Executive Powers, [Sec. 2 and 3.]
  - 3. Subject to Impeachment. [Sec. 4.]
- III. **Judicial Department**; [Art. III.]
  - 1. (1) Courts, (2) Term of Office, (3) Salary, [Sec. 1.]
  - 2. Jurisdiction, [Sec. 2.]
  - 3. Treason. [Sec. 3.]

---

* This logically does not belong to the division "The National Government," but to "Miscellaneous Provisions," but it is thought best to retain the order of

MISCELLANEOUS PROVISIONS.

I. RELATIONS OF STATES; [Art. IV.]
  1. Records of one State in another, [Sec. 1.]
  2. Rights in one State of Citizens of another, [Sec. 2.]
  3. (1) New States, (2) U. S. Territory, [Sec. 3.]
  4. Protection of States by Nation. [Sec. 4.]

II. AMENDMENT. [Art. V.]

III. (1) **NATIONAL DEBT**; (2) **NATIONAL SUPREMACY**; (3) **OATH**. [Art. VI.]

IV. ESTABLISHMENT OF CONSTITUTION. [Art. VII].

II. AMENDMENTS.

1. Arts. I.–VIII. Prohibitions on Congress as to Personal Rights.
2. Arts. IX. and X. Rights not named in Constitution.
3. Art. XI. Judicial Jurisdiction.
4. Art. XII. Election of President and Vice-President.
5. Art. XIII. Abolition of Slavery.
6. Art. XIV. (1) Equal Civil Rights, (2) Apportionment of Representatives, (3) Political Disabilities, (4) Public Debt.
7. Art. XV. Right of Suffrage.

---

the Constitution itself. There are some other cases where the true logical order is not followed in the Constitution. The provisions regarding the choosing of officers and impeachment in sections 2 and 3 of Article I. would more properly come in section 5, as they relate to certain powers of the Houses. That regarding revenue bills in section 7 would properly fall in the following section, as it relates to the law-making powers of Congress.

SECTION II.

LEGISLATIVE DEPARTMENT.

CHAPTER XXV.

HOUSE OF REPRESENTATIVES.

1. Preamble.—The preamble is an important part of the Constitution. The object of the Constitution was to remedy the defects existing under the Confederation, and some of the clauses of the preamble refer to those defects (**1**).* We have seen that the Union then was a very imperfect one. Instead of there being "domestic tranquillity" the States were continually quarrelling. It was impossible to "provide for the common defence" of the country against foreign enemies, or to "promote the general welfare" by broad measures, unless there were a strong central government. Had the Constitution not been adopted and had the States remained independent, it is not probable that the country would have had the unexampled prosperity that it has.

2. Congress.—This is the name of the national legislative body, and like the state legislatures it is divided into two Houses, called the Senate and House of Representatives (**2**). The former represents the States, and the latter the people. The members of the House,† called

---

* These numbers refer to the paragraphs of the Constitution. The pupil should turn back to it at each reference.

† The House of Representatives is frequently called simply the "House" w]

Representatives, are elected by the people of the States every second year (3). Members of the Congress under the Confederation were appointed by the state legislatures, and for one year.

3. **Electors.**—There was much discussion and difference of opinion in the Convention as to what should be the qualifications of the voters who should elect the Representatives. The qualifications of electors were various in the different States. In some of them owners of property, or tax-payers, in others freeholders* only, were voters. In some, only the latter voted for the higher officers; in a few, suffrage was almost universal. Finally, as a compromise, it was decided that the qualifications should be the same in each State as those requisite for electors of its lower house, as it was presumed no State would object to such a rule (3).

4. **Qualifications.**—A Representative must be twenty-five years of age, must have been a citizen seven years, and must live in the State from which he is chosen (4). The reasons for this will be readily understood. If voters must have certain qualifications, surely those who make laws for them should have higher ones. (See Chap. V.)

5. **Number.**—The Constitution does not limit the House to any definite number of Representatives; it only declares that the number shall not exceed one for every 30,000 inhabitants. Otherwise it might become too large. It requires an enumeration of the inhabitants every ten years; and the next Congress thereafter determines the ratio of representation† and the number of Representatives, and apportions them among the States (5).

6. **Present Number.**—The first House of Representatives

---

* A freeholder is one owning land, either absolutely or during his own or some one else's life.

† The word *ratio* signifies rate, or proportion. It here means the number of   3.

consisted of sixty-five members, and the ratio was about one to every 50,000 inhabitants. Since then, as the population has increased, Congress has increased the ratio, in order that the House might not grow too large to transact business, but in spite of that the House has grown, until now (1883) it consists of three hundred and twenty-five members, being about one for every 150,000.

7. **Every State Represented.**—But it might happen (and has happened) that some States would not have a population equal to the ratio. In view of this the Constitution provides that no State shall lose its representation in the House, by declaring that each State shall have at least one Representative (5).

8. **Apportionment.**—With regard to how many Representatives the different States should have the Convention found it difficult to agree. In the Congress under the Confederation, it will be remembered, the States were entitled to an equal number of delegates, and each State had one vote. But now it was proposed to apportion the Representatives according to population. On this point there were two causes of contention. First: The small States opposed it, because it gave them fewer Representatives, and therefore less power in Congress. The large States insisted on it, saying that they ought to have greater power because they had greater interests. Finally the small States yielded with regard to the House of Representatives. Second: The slaveholding (Southern) States claimed that, in reckoning the population for the purpose of apportioning Representatives, slaves should be included; the *non-slaveholding (Northern) States* insisted that only free persons should

---

* Slavery then existed in all the States except Massachusetts; but as there were very few slaves in the Northern States, they are generally spoken of as if they were at that time non-slaveholding States.

be included, as the slaves could not vote themselves, and it was unjust to give the free persons extra votes simply because they owned certain property—that being what slaves were considered. The controversy on this point rose so high, and the parties were for a long time so unyielding, that fears were entertained of a sudden dissolution of the Convention.

9. Result.—The result was a compromise. The Northern States finally consented that three-fifths of the slaves [the words "all other persons" in section 2 (5) mean slaves] should be counted, and the Southern States consented that direct taxes should be laid on the same basis; so that the Southern States would have the larger share of Representatives, but would pay the larger share of direct taxes.* But, as it resulted, the advantage, contrary to anticipation, was almost wholly on the side of the Southern States, for very few direct taxes were laid before the late Civil War, and thus they obtained the increased representation without the corresponding increase in taxation.

10. Present Rule.—The state of things described in the last section with regard to apportionment existed up to the Civil War. The 13th, 14th, and 15th Amendments changed the system. Now Representatives are apportioned

---

* To illustrate this rule by an example: Suppose a State contained 600,000 free persons and 500,000 slaves. Adding three-fifths of the number of slaves (300,000) to the number of free persons gives 900,000 as the number of the representative population: and the State would have been entitled to *three* Representatives for every *two* that a State which contained 600,000 free inhabitants and no slaves would have. So in apportioning taxes according to population, the State in the case we have supposed would have been obliged to raise *three* dollars for every *two* that it would have been obliged to raise if no slaves had been counted.

in proportion to the total population, whether white or black (**100**).*

11. Territories.—By an act of Congress, every Territory in which a government has been established is entitled to send a delegate to Congress, who has a right to take part in the debates of the House, but not the right of voting there.

CHAPTER XXVI.

SENATE.

1. Reasons for Two Houses.—In this country and in England it is thought best that the legislative body should consist of two houses. If there were only one house it might pass some very harmful or unjust laws, either through undue haste, ignorance, popular excitement, or the undue influence of popular but mistaken leaders. But if there were another house, it would be improbable that the very same influences should exist in both, and thus one house would correct the hasty legislation of the other. And if one house were of a higher grade than the other, composed of wiser men, it is seen that its restrictive influence would be of the greater value.

2. Character of Senate.—For these reasons the Constitution has established the Senate, and has made it a body of greater dignity than the House of Representatives. The causes which make the Senate the more select body are four in number: (1) it has fewer members; (2) they are

---

* The number of Indians not taxed is so small that it need not be considered.

elected by the State legislatures instead of by the people; (3) the term of office is longer; and (4) the qualifications are higher.

3. **State Equality.**—In the Senate the States are equal in power, each having two members (**8**). The Convention readily agreed upon dividing Congress into two branches; but, as has been observed, it was difficult to settle the mode of representation. The delegates from the large States insisted upon a representation in proportion to population, in the Senate as well as in the House; and the small States contended for equality in both branches. The debate was long and animated; and it became apparent that, as in the case of slave representation in the House, there must be a compromise. This was at length effected; the small States consenting to a proportional representation in the House, and the large States to an equal representation in the Senate.* Thus while the House represents the people, the Senate represents the States, and this is one instance in which the federation principle is retained. (See page 100, sec. 7.)

4. **Voting.**—In the Congress under the Confederation the voting was by States, but the Senate differs in that respect. There the Senators vote separately, the vote of each Senator counting one, as in the House; and a question is decided by the united votes of a majority of the members, and not by the vote of a majority of the States (**8**).

5. **Term.**—The period of six years was also the result of a compromise in the Convention (**8**). The terms pro-

---

* It will be noticed that in the Convention which framed the Constitution there were many opposing interests, and that compromises were frequently necessary, each State giving up something. It was a spirit of patriotism which caused this, as well as the instinct of self-preservation, for without compromise no permanent union could have been formed, saving the rights of all.

posed varied from three to nine years, or even longer. One object in making it longer than a Representative's term was to obtain a body of men wiser and more experienced than the House would contain. Where a man is to be elected for a long term greater care will be used in selecting him. A second object was to obtain independence of popular impulses. The Representatives were to reflect the will of the people, and so it was provided that they might be often changed: but the Senators were to serve as a check upon hasty action by the people's representatives, and for this purpose they must feel independent of the people to a certain degree. A long term tends to give this independence. A third object was to check frequent changes in the laws. The oftener a legislature is changed the more changeable and uncertain will be the laws; and uncertainty and change often do more injury than evil laws.

6. Gradual Change.—Senators are not all elected at the same time. One-third go out of office every two years (**9**). In favor of this arrangement are two important considerations. First: It secures to the public at all times the benefit of the experience of at least two-thirds of the body. Whereas, if the terms of all the Senators expired at once, their places might be supplied mainly by new members without the requisite knowledge and experience. Second: While a long term is intended to guard against the too frequent changes in the laws, it may also prevent, for too long a time, the amendment or the repeal of bad laws. Such amendment or repeal may be hastened by the election of new members in the place of the one-third who retire every two years.

7. Qualifications.—Why these are higher than in the case of Representatives has been explained (see sec. 2). An additional reason for requiring them to have been citizens of the United States nine years is found in the fact that, with the President, they make treaties with foreign nations **(62)**. A Senator should therefore have lived here long enough to have become free from bias in favor of his native country.

CHAPTER XXVII.

GENERAL LEGISLATIVE REGULATIONS.*

1. Choice of Officers.—It is considered important in legislative bodies that each house should have the choice of its own officers, in order that it may have proper control of them. A Speaker not responsible to the House of Representatives (e g. if appointed by the President) might baffle the will of the entire House. One exception to this rule is that the Vice-President presides in the Senate. The States follow this by having the Lieutenant-Governor preside in the state senate **(7, 12)**.

2. Impeachment.—Impeachment and its trial have been described before (see page 79). As in the state legislatures, so in Congress, the lower House impeaches and the upper House tries. The officers subject to impeachment by the national House of Representatives are the President, Vice-President, and all civil officers of the United States (not of any State) **(65)**. This means all members of the civil (i.e. not military), executive and judicial departments of the Nation. Thus neither members of Congress nor of the army or navy can be removed in this way. In practice only officials of the highest rank are ever impeached.

---

* Most of the provisions contained in sections 4, 5, 6, and 7 of Article I. will be easily understood, and many of them are similar to provisions in the state constitutions. We will speak only of a few which requ

3. **Meetings of Congress.**—Congress meets every year, in December **(16)**. But as every second year the entire House of Representatives and one-third of the Senate are elected anew, the two sessions following an election are classed together and called "A Congress." The meeting of Congress in December 1881 was the first session of the 47th Congress.

4. **Rules.**—Like state legislatures each House of Congress has its rules, which in most cases are strictly followed. A bill is introduced, referred to its appropriate committee, reported by the committee, read, debated, and passed (or rejected), in substantially the same manner as in state legislatures (see page 42). But at any time either House may set aside all its rules, and pass laws in any manner it sees fit, provided no provision of the Constitution is violated.

5. **Salary.**—In the Convention there was much discussion as to whether it would be wise to allow salaries to members of Congress. On the one hand it was said salaries would tempt unworthy men to intrigue for an election; on the other hand, the worthiest men might be shut out through poverty if no compensation were allowed. It was decided to allow compensation. The amount is fixed by Congress itself **(21)**.

6. **Arrest of Members.**—Members of Congress (except in certain cases) cannot be arrested when Congress is in session **(21)**. This is in order that the people who elect them may not be deprived of their services.

7. **Liberty of Speech.**—The clause which says that a member "shall not be questioned in any other place" for any speech, means that he shall not be sued, either civilly or criminally, for anything he says in debate **(21)**. This is in order that members may feel the fullest freedom and independence.

8. **Revenue Bills.**—These are bills for raising money for the government, either by direct or indirect taxation. All other laws may originate in either House, but these must be passed by the House of Representatives first (**23**). The reason for this is that since the people pay the taxes, it is appropriate that the Representatives elected directly by them should propose all such laws.

9. **Veto.**—But a bill having passed both Houses is not yet a law. It must be presented to the President, who is thus a part of the legislative department. There are three ways in which a bill, after having passed both Houses, may become a law: (1) it may be signed by the President; (2) he may neglect to sign it for ten days; and (3) he may return it to Congress within ten days, and each House may pass it a second time by a two-thirds vote (**24, 25**).

CHAPTER XXVIII.

POWERS OF TAXATION.

1. **Nature of the National Government.**—Before treating of the several legislative powers we will first speak of a certain characteristic of the General Government in which it differs from the States, and which must be always kept in mind when considering its law-making powers. The United States Government is a government of *delegated* powers; that is, powers which have been *delegated* to it by the States, or the people of the States. It has only such powers as the People have given it, in the Constitution. Hence it is called a government of *limited* powers. The States, on the other hand, existing before the General Gov-

ernment, and possessing entire sovereignty, at least in theory, may exercise all powers which they have not surrendered to the General Government. In other words, their powers are *unlimited*, except so far as they have parted with any of their original powers. Therefore, when the question arises whether the President or Congress have certain powers, we look in the Constitution, and if they are not there granted, they do not exist. But when the question arises, with regard to a State, whether its people have a certain power, we approach it from the other side and say they have the power unless the United States Constitution has taken it away. Most of the legislative powers of Congress are enumerated in Article I., section 8. The first one grants the power to tax (**26**).

2. Necessity for the Taxing Power.—This is one of the most important powers of government. A government without the power to raise money hardly deserves the name. Without money it would have no power to enforce obedience to its laws, for it could not pay soldiers or civil officers, and men will not serve without pay. We have seen how the Confederation tried the experiment and failed.* This was one of its errors, corrected in the Constitution.

3. Manner of Taxation.—Taxes † may be laid by the

---

* See page 95.

† The four words, *taxes, duties, imposts,* and *excises*, are not used to mean four different things, but only to cover all the usual methods of taxation. These words have not fixed meanings. Some of them have different meanings in different connections. At times some have the same meaning as others. Their most usual meanings when used in connection with one another are perhaps these: *taxes*, direct taxes laid on individuals, either as poll taxes, or taxes in proportion to property (see Chap. XV., for distinction between direct and indirect taxes); *duties*, indirect taxes of all kinds, including taxes on exports, imports, and excises; *imposts*, duties on imports; *excises*, duties on goods manufactured and used here. Another word *customs* usually

General Government in three ways: (1) upon persons directly, as poll or property taxes; (2) upon goods when they are imported into the country from abroad, or (3) upon goods when they are manufactured and used here. This clause **(26)** would also grant the power to lay export duties—that is, duties to be paid on goods when sent from this to foreign countries—did not a later provision forbid it **(48)**.

4. Objects.—The objects for which taxes may be laid are also enumerated in the same clause **(26)**. Since it is the theory of the Constitution that Congress shall have power over only those matters which affect the whole country, leaving all local matters to the States, so no tax can be laid except for some purpose of interest to all the people of the Nation. But the phrase "general welfare" is very broad.

5. Uniformity.—The Constitution is careful to provide that no State shall pay more than its just share of taxes. There are several provisions regulating this. First, direct taxes must be laid in proportion to population **(5, 98)**; second, all indirect taxes which may be laid (i.e. imposts and excises) must be uniform throughout the country **(26)**; third, no export duties can be laid **(48)**. The reasons for the last provision are that a tariff * of export duties which would bear equally on the States would be very difficult to make, since they do not export the same

---

means duties on imports and exports, but in this country, since there are no export duties, it usually means the same as *imposts*.

Duties are *specific* and *ad valorem*. A *specific* duty is a specified sum of money charged upon every yard, pound, or gallon of any commodity. Thus, a duty of ten cents on a pound of tea, or of one dollar on a yard of cloth, or of fifty cents on a gallon of wine, is a specific duty. *Ad valorem* is a Latin phrase, signifying *according to the value*. An *ad valorem* duty is a certain *percentage* on the value or price.

* A *tariff* means a list of duties laid.

articles, some exporting cotton, others grain, and others manufactures, and that it would constitute a constant cause of irritation between the States. For instance, the Representatives of the cotton and grain States might combine and pass a law laying very low duties on cotton and grain and high ones on manufactures.

6. Taxes which have been laid.—Up to the late Civil War very few direct taxes had been laid by the National Government. They were then laid for a few years, but now (1882) there are none. Some excise duties have been and are now laid, chiefly on liquors and tobacco, articles that are not necessary to the people, but are luxuries. During the Civil War the excise duties collected were about equal to the customs. But from the beginning very many duties on imports have been laid, and it is from this source that most of the revenue has been raised.

7. Power to Borrow Money.—This is given to Congress for the reasons already described, which justify state debts (page 71, sec. 7) **(27)**. This power was exercised during the war until the national debt nearly reached the sum of $3,000,000,000. Without this power the government would have been almost helpless, for its regular income would have been wholly inadequate.

CHAPTER XXIX.

POWER TO REGULATE COMMERCE (28).

1. Why given to Congress.—This was for two reasons: (1) because it was a matter of general and universal interest, and (2) because of the benefits that would flow from uniformity. The need of no power was more deeply felt under the Confederation than the power to regulate foreign trade. We thus see that the power to lay duties comes from two clauses. One **(26)** gives Congress the power, but only for purposes of revenue. If none should be needed for that purpose, or if the duties laid for revenue were not sufficient to regulate commerce, they might be laid under the other clause **(28)** to any amount.

2. **Nature of Regulation.**—This regulation is of two kinds: (1) the laying of duties on goods imported from abroad, for the purpose of protecting the commercial interests of this country; and (2) making regulations which shall tend to render navigation less dangerous. The manner and object of regulating commerce by means of import duties will be seen if we consider the trade of England and America as it was after the Revolution.

3. **Retaliatory Duties.**—England pursued the policy, for her own benefit, of laying heavy duties on merchandise imported there from this country. That injured us, and so, in order to compel her to abandon the policy, we wished to lay duties on articles sent here by the English merchants.*

---

* The effect of these duties may not be quite clear: Suppose the market value of a bushel of wheat in Great Britain to be $1, and the cost of raising the article here and carrying it there to be (together) $1. We can then raise it here and sell it there along with the English producer. If now a duty of 40 cents a bushel is laid upon wheat from abroad, we cannot sell it for less than $1.40, and the English consumer, instead of buying it with this duty added, will buy of the English producer. But, the people of this country being then chiefly agricultural, more wheat was produced here than there was a market for, and the American farmer was dependent on the foreign markets. Being shut out of the English market, the value of our products fell, and we suffered loss. It was thought then that if we retaliated and laid duties on manufactured articles (of which England sent us a great number), and so shut them out, she would be influenced to abandon her duties.

Under the Confederation this was attempted, but as each State could lay what duties it chose, there was no uniformity, and each would try to secure the trade by laying lower duties than the rest. So the Constitution gave Congress exclusive authority over the whole subject, and retaliatory duties were laid.

4. Protection.—Another way in which it was thought duties on imports would protect the commercial interests of the country was in encouraging and protecting the manufacturing interests.* This theory is called *protection*, and is the policy which the country has followed. High protective duties have been laid almost from the beginning on articles manufactured from cotton, wool, and iron.

5. Free Trade.—But it is believed by many that protection is a mistaken policy, at least in this country at present, and that while it encourages manufactures it injures some other interests. The opposing policy is called *free trade*. Its supporters urge that if the yard of cloth can be brought here and sold for less than it can be made here, the people who pay for it lose by shutting it out, and the few manufacturers are the only ones who gain.† The English Government now acts on the policy of free trade.

---

* Suppose foreign cloth of a certain quality is sold in this country for $2.50 a yard, and cloth of the same quality manufactured here cannot be made for less than $3 a yard. There would now be no encouragement to any one to engage in the manufacture of such cloth, because, in order to sell it, he must reduce the price to that of the foreign article, which would subject him to a loss of fifty cents a yard. Let now a duty of $1 a yard be laid upon the foreign cloth, and the price would be $3.50, and preference would be given to the domestic article, unless the importer should reduce the price of his foreign cloth to $3; in which case, it is to be presumed, about an equal quantity of each would be consumed, and the duty of $1 a yard on the foreign cloth would go into the United States Treasury

† [The reviser of this book believes that free trade is the juster

6. Collection of Duties.—Certain places on the coast are designated by the laws of Congress, called *ports of entry*, and a vessel must first come to one of these, where the master delivers a statement of the cargo to an officer, appointed by the President, called a *collector of customs*. The cargo is then examined, and the duties calculated and paid to the collector. If not paid the collector seizes the goods, which are forfeited to the government.

7. Registry.—Another regulation of commerce is that by which a vessel built and owned in this country may be *registered* on the collector's books as an American vessel. As such it has certain privileges which foreign vessels do not have. A foreign vessel is not allowed to engage in the coast trade here. An American vessel, registered, is in all places entitled to the full protection of our government, and if it is taken or injured by foreigners in foreign waters the United States Government must demand reparation from the government to which they belong.

8. Clearance and Entry.—Every time a vessel (foreign or domestic) leaves a port, what is called a *clearance* must be obtained. This is a certificate by the collector that all the fees upon the vessel have been paid, and the law been complied with in all respects. So when a vessel arrives at a port, the master must report its arrival to the collector of the port, deliver up a statement of its cargo and the clearance he received at the port from which he came. This is called *entering* the vessel.*

9. Navigation Laws.—Coming now to the second class of regulations of commerce, Congress has passed many laws

---

and better policy for all nations. But there is much to be said on each side of the question, as it is a rather intricate one, and this is not the place for such a discussion.]

* In the coasting trade between ports of the United States, clearance and entry are not required, in general.

to render navigation less dangerous. The following are some of the subjects: providing for light-houses, buoys, signal stations, and life-saving stations along the coast; improving harbors; requiring vessels to take licensed pilots when near the coast; prescribing how many passengers and what provisions shall be carried; quarantine;* and many similar ones.

10. **Commerce with Indians.**—In granting to Congress the power to regulate commerce† "with the Indian tribes," it was intended to lessen the dangers of war. Murders and war had been provoked by the improper conduct of some of the States. It was believed that by a uniform policy difficulties would be more likely to be prevented. This was more important then than now, when the number of Indians has become so insignificant.

CHAPTER XXX.

OTHER POWERS RELATING TO PEACE.

1. Citizens and Aliens.—The general distinction between them is this: *citizens* are those born in this country; ‡

---

* This means a period of time for which vessels are detained before entering a port, so that they may be examined to see if there is any malignant disease on board. Quarantines are required by the health laws of the States; and by the laws of Congress vessels are to be subject to the health laws of the State at whose ports they arrive.

† Commerce, in a broad sense, as used in this clause of the Constitution, means not only trade by sea and land, but all intercourse.

‡ Prior to the Civil War white people alone were citizens in the Southern States, but now under the 14th Amendment white and black stand on the same basis (99).

Children take the citizenship of their parents.

aliens are those born in a foreign country, whether living here or in the foreign country. Both include men, women, and children. But after living here a certain time an alien may become a citizen. Aliens have not all the rights of citizens. They cannot vote (see page 27).*
In many States they have not full power to own real estate. In general, they are considered subjects of the nation from which they come, and not of this.

2. Naturalization.—But to deny foreigners the rights of citizens after they shall have acquired a fixed residence here, and a knowledge of their civil and political duties, would be illiberal and unjust. The process by which an alien may become a citizen is called *naturalization*. Congress has the power to make a uniform rule **(29)**. The reason for this is that if it were left to the States, a person having become naturalized in one State might, on removing into another, be deprived of the rights of citizenship until he should have been naturalized by the laws of such State. Besides, by the Constitution a citizen of any State is entitled to the privileges of a citizen in any other State **(73)**. Now, after a person is once naturalized, he is a citizen of the United States and also of the State in which he resides at the time **(99)**. By removing to another he becomes a citizen of that.

3. When Allowed.—The laws of Congress prescribe that an alien may be naturalized after living in this country five years. The first step is to declare on oath before a court that it is his intention to become a citizen. This declara-

---

* Naturalization and the right to vote are two separate matters, which must not be confused. Not all of those who are naturalized are given the right to vote (e.g. women and children). Although most States do give foreigners the right to vote, when naturalized, still they need not; and some States even allow some aliens to vote. The State regulates voting, the United States naturalization.

tion he may make as soon as he arrives, or at any time. After the declaration he must wait two years. After that the court, if satisfied that he has resided five years in the United States, and one year in the State in which the court is held, may admit him as a citizen. He then, before the court, renounces his allegiance to his old country, and swears to support the Constitution of the United States. But no alien can be compelled to become a citizen against his will.

4. Bankrupt Laws.—A *bankrupt* is an insolvent debtor; that is, a person who is unable to pay all his just debts. A *bankrupt law* is a law which, upon an insolvent's giving up all his property to his creditors, discharges him from the payment of his debts. Such laws are designed for the benefit of honest and unfortunate debtors, who, by having the enjoyment of their future earnings secured to them, are encouraged to engage anew in industrial pursuits. The reason the power was given to Congress to pass such laws (**29**) was that if it were left to the States the object could not be accomplished. No state law could release a debtor from debts to a creditor living out of the State, nor from debts contracted in another State. The dissimilar and conflicting laws of the different States, and the entire want of them in others, had caused great inconvenience. Important as such laws were deemed, there is now (1880) no national law on the subject.*

5. Coinage.—The coinage of the money is in every country a prerogative of the government. Congress has several powers with regard to coinage (**30**). No State can

---

* Three such laws have been passed by Congress. Two of them existed but a year or two. The third was passed in 1867 and lasted until 1878. The reason for this short duration was the general sentiment that it allowed many dishonest debtors to procure a release from their debts.

coin money (**51**). The object here, also, was to make uniformity throughout the country. Exercising these powers Congress has passed laws by which we have a uniform currency throughout the Nation, and the convenient decimal system of dollars and cents, instead of the awkward system of pounds, shillings, and pence, which existed before the Constitution. The value of coin has been regulated in different ways: such as, by deciding how much metal (gold or silver) shall be put in a given coin, or what domestic coins foreign coins shall be equal to. The place where money* is coined is called a *mint*. There are several in the country, the principal one being at Philadelphia.

    6. **Weights and Measures.**—For the convenience of trade between the States, the weights and measures, like the coinage, should be the same in all the States. Without such uniformity commerce among the States would meet with very great embarrassment. Yet Congress has never exercised the power given it on this subject (**30**). The States still have the power to adopt their own standard.†

    7. **Post-Office.**—The power of Congress over the mail is one of the most important it has (**32**).‡ In every nation

---

    * It must be remembered that coin is not the only money in the country. We have, besides, all the paper money now in use (1880), United States notes, national-bank notes, and state-bank bills. Only coin and the United States notes are legal tender, i.e. if a man wishes to pay a debt he must pay with one of those two, if the creditor insists upon it.

    † The weights and measures used throughout the States are, however, substantially the same. In 1836 the United States Government sent to each State a full set of weights and measures, as used in the Custom House, and these have been adopted by the States as their standards.

    ‡ A post-road is a road over which the mail is carried. All railroads are by law made post-roads, and there are very many others besides.

the government assumes charge of the Post-office. It is impossible to conceive all the difficulties which might attend the exercise of this power had it been left to the different States. A uniform system of regulations is indispensable to efficiency, and could be secured only by placing this power in the hands of Congress.

8. Protection of Authors and Inventors.—This Congress has power to effect by granting *copyrights* and *patents* (**33**). "Science and useful arts" are promoted by new books and new inventions. But if every man had the right to print and sell every book or writing, without compensation to the author, there would be little to encourage men of ability to spend, as is often done, years of labor in preparing new and useful works. Nor would men of genius be likely to spend their time and money in inventing and constructing expensive machinery, if others had an equal right to make and sell the same. This power is given to Congress for the reason that if the States alone exercised it, no State could punish infringers beyond its own limits. In pursuance of the power here given, Congress has enacted the copyright and patent laws.

9. Copyright.—A *copyright* is the sole right to print and sell a book, map, etc. It is obtained by the author by following a few simple requirements, the chief one of which is the mailing of two copies as soon as it is published to the Librarian of Congress. This secures to the author the sole right to print and sell his work anywhere in the United States for twenty-eight years, at the expiration of which time he may have his right continued for fourteen years longer.

10. Patents.—A *patent* is the sole right to make, use, or sell a new invention. It is obtained by the inventor from the government, but there is much more to be done than in the case of a copyright. The Commissioner of Patents superintends the granting of patents. The Patent Office is a part of the Department of the Interior (see page 169). To secure his patent the inventor must send to the Commissioner of Patents a written description of his invention, with drawings and model, and specify the improvement which he claims as his own discovery. If the examiners do not find that the invention had been before discovered, a patent is issued therefor, on the payment of certain fees. This secures to the inventor the sole right to make, sell, or use his invention anywhere in the United States for seventeen years.*

11. Courts.—Under the power to establish inferior courts (**34**) Congress has established a system of courts which will be described later (see page 171).

12. Piracy.—Congress (and not the States) has power to define and punish crimes committed on the high seas (**35**). *Piracy* is commonly defined to be forcible robbery or depredation upon the high seas. But the term *felony* was not exactly defined by law, consequently its meaning was not the same in all the States. It was sometimes applied to capital offences only; at other times, to all crimes above misdemeanors. The power to define these offences is given to Congress for the sake of uniformity, and the power to punish them, because the States have no jurisdiction beyond their own limits.

13. Offences against the Law of Nations.—Nor were these clearly defined. The power to define and punish them is given to Congress (**35**), because our citizens are

---

* In the case of both copyrights and patents, the granting of them is not proof that the book or invention is new. If any one is sued for infringement (i.e. printing the book or using the invention without permission from the one holding the copyright or patent) he may claim that the book or the invention is not new, and if he proves it the court adjudges the copyright or patent to be void.

regarded by foreign nations as citizens of the United States and not as citizens of their respective States; and therefore the General Government alone is responsible to foreign nations for injuries committed on the high seas by our citizens.

14. District of Columbia.—In 1790 this became the seat of government. Over it, and over all the forts, arsenals, etc., belonging to the United States, Congress has exclusive authority* **(42)**. This authority is necessary for the protection of the government. If the seat of government were within the jurisdiction of a State, Congress and other public officers would be dependent on the state authority for protection in the discharge of their duties, and the State might refuse them protection.†

15. Implied Powers.—It is a general rule that where one is granted the power to do a thing, it implies that he shall have power to use all the necessary means to accomplish it. The last clause of section 8 **(43)** then was unnecessary, for the granting of the "foregoing powers" granted also the power "to make laws necessary and proper for carrying them into execution." ‡ The reason the clause was added

---

* So also with regard to all territory not included within any State (see page 180).

† This actually happened to the Continental Congress. It was once, near the close of the Revolution, treated with insult and abuse while sitting at Philadelphia; and the executive authority of Pennsylvania having failed to afford protection, it adjourned to Princeton, in the State of New Jersey

‡ For example: The power "to regulate commerce" includes the power to cause the construction of breakwaters and light-houses, the removal of obstructions from navigable rivers, and the improvement of harbors; for in regulating and facilitating commerce these works and improvements are necessary. So the power "to establish post-offices" implies the power to punish persons for robbing the mail

was to satisfy all possible doubt. Under this right of implied powers Congress has passed laws which it has been difficult to refer to their proper clauses in the Constitution, and which have occasioned much discussion; such as laws establishing the national banks, incorporating railroads, purchasing foreign territory (such as Louisiana and Florida) and making the United States notes legal tender. In very many cases the laws passed under implied powers are wider in their scope and more important than those expressly authorized.

16. Other Powers.—In other parts of the Constitution other legislative powers are given to Congress. They will be noticed in their order.

CHAPTER XXXI.

POWERS RELATING TO WAR.

1. Declaring War.—Congress alone has this right (36). It is very evident that a single State ought not to be allowed to make war. The power to declare it is justly given to the National Government, because the people of all the States become involved in its evils. In monarchical governments this important power is exercised by the king, or supreme ruler. But here it is entrusted—not to the President—but to the representatives of the people, because the people are they who have to bear the burdens of war.

2. Letters of Marque and Reprisal.—These are commissions issued by a government to private persons authorizing them to seize the property of a foreign nation or its subjects, as a reparation for some injury.* Congress has exclusive power to grant them **(36, 51)**. A State should not be permitted to authorize its citizens to make reprisals; for, although such authority, when granted in time of peace, is designed to enable the citizens of one country to obtain redress for injuries committed by those of another, without a resort to war, the tendency of reprisals is to provoke rather than to prevent war; and when granted in time of war it is merely one means of carrying on the war. In both cases the National Government alone should have the power to grant the commissions, as it alone has the power to declare war, because the whole country may become involved. The entire subject of war is taken away from the States, and given to the Nation.

3. Captures.—As a part of its power over war, Congress has power to make rules concerning the property captured in time of war. The general practice is to distribute the proceeds of the property among the captors as a reward for bravery and a stimulus to exertion. The property captured is called *prize*. But proof must be made in a court of the United States that the property was taken from the enemy, before it is condemned by the court as a prize.

4. Army and Navy.—So also Congress has power to raise, maintain, and make rules for the government of an

---

* They are sometimes called simply *letters of marque*, and are often issued in time of war, and sometimes in time of peace. When issued, it is generally to the owners or master of some armed vessel, which then goes out and captures the vessels and property of the foreign nation on the ocean. Such a vessel is called a *privateer* (see page 268).

This method of obtaining reparation seems more like retaliation. But many things are allowed in war which are not justifiable at other times. Privateering is not as extensively practised as formerly.

army and navy (**37-40**).* Under the Confederation the Congress could declare war, but could not raise or pay a single soldier (see page 94). A government must have an army, or at least the power to raise one. Without one it is virtually powerless, for not only must a nation be ready to fight foreign foes, but also occasions will arise when its supremacy can be maintained against insurrections or rebellions among its own subjects in no other way. So also maritime nations must have a navy to protect their commerce. In ordinary times the United States army and navy are filled by voluntary *enlistments*, but when these do not furnish enough men Congress provides for a *conscription*, called during our late war a *draft*. By this the number needed are chosen by lot from among the citizens, and they are compelled to go, or furnish a substitute. In order that Congress shall not lose control of the army when raised, it is provided that no appropriation shall be made for a longer period than two years. It may, however, make as many successive appropriations as it sees fit, and they are now made every year for such year.

5. **Militia.**—Congress also can provide for calling out the militia (**40**). It has so provided by delegating the power to the President, to be so exercised when he thinks the necessity provided for by the Constitution has arisen.†

---

* The policy of the country has been to maintain a very small army and navy, and undoubtedly much of our prosperity, as compared with other nations, is due to this. In European nations not only do the people have to bear the burden of an immense standing army, but in many of them several years of the best part of every man's life must be spent in service.

† Though the President is Commander-in-Chief of the army, navy, and militia, Congress still has practical control of all, for before they can be paid Congress must raise the money and appropriate it (**49**). In ordinary times this is done every year.

EXPRESS POWERS OF CONGRESS.

[Under Art. I. sec. 8.]

I. ORDINARY PEACE POWERS.

I. RAISING MONEY;
  1. By Levying,
      { 1. Direct Taxes,   } For the { 1. Payment of Debts,
      { 2. Imposts, or   } purpose { 2. Common Defence, or
      { 3. Excises: } of   { 3. General Welfare.
  2. By Borrowing.

II. COMMERCE, REGULATION OF;
  1. Foreign,
  2. Among States, and
  3. With Indians.

III. NATURALIZATION.

IV. BANKRUPTCY.

V. COINAGE;
  1. Coining Money,
  2. Regulation of Value, of
      { 1. Domestic Coin, and
      { 2. Foreign Coin.

VI. WEIGHTS AND MEASURES, REGULATION OF.

VII. POST-OFFICE; Establishment of
  1. Post-Offices, and
  2. Post-Roads.

VIII. SCIENCE AND USEFUL ARTS, ENCOURAGEMENT OF,
by granting
- 1. Copyrights, and
- 2. Patents.

IX. INFERIOR COURTS, ESTABLISHMENT OF.

X. CRIMES;
- 1. Piracies,
- 2. Felonies on High Seas, } to { 1. Define, and
- 3. International Offences, } { 2. Punish.
- 4. Counterfeiting ;............to punish.
  - 1. U. S. Securities, and
  - 2. U. S. Coin.

XI. TERRITORY; EXCLUSIVE LEGISLATION OVER
- 1. District of Columbia, and
- 2. Forts, etc.

II. POWERS RELATING TO WAR.

I. DECLARATION OF WAR,

II. LETTERS OF MARQUE, GRANTING OF,

III. CAPTURES, RULES CONCERNING,

IV. FORCES;
- 1. Army, } to { 1. Raise,
- 2. Navy, } { 2. Maintain, and
- { 3. Make Rules for.
- 3. Militia, to Provide for
  - 1. Calling out, to
    - 1. Execute Laws,
    - 2. Suppress Insurrections, or
    - 3. Repel Invasions.
  - 2. Organizing,
  - 3. Arming, } at all times.
  - 4. Disciplining, and }
  - 5. Governing,   when in U. S. service.

CHAPTER XXXII.

PROHIBITIONS ON THE UNITED STATES.

1. Where Found.—Section 9 of Article I. names certain subjects which Congress is forbidden to legislate upon.* Most of these form exceptions to the powers granted in the preceding section.

2. Slave-Trade.—From an early period slaves had been imported into the Colonies from Africa. At the time when the Constitution was formed, laws prohibiting the foreign slave-trade had been passed in most of the States, but the delegates from a few States in the Convention insisted on having the privilege of importing slaves secured. A majority of the Convention were in favor of leaving Congress free to prohibit the trade at any time. But as it was doubtful whether certain States would in such case accede to the Constitution, and as it was desirable to bring as many States as possible into the Union, it was at length agreed that the trade should be left free for twenty years to all the States choosing to continue it **(44, 79)**. Once more, a compromise.†

3. Habeas Corpus.—The nature of this writ has been heretofore explained (see page 85). The presence of this clause **(45)** here shows how important the writ was considered. In England its operation had at times been sus-

---

* It must be remembered that sec. 9 of Art. I. does not apply to the States, but only to Congress. The prohibitions upon the States are found in sec. 10. For instance, a state legislature is not prohibited by the United States Constitution from suspending the writ of habeas corpus, as far as state offences are concerned. For this reason provisions similar to those in sec. 9 are generally found in state constitutions, as to habeas corpus, appropriations, statements, etc

† Congr   adc.

pended for slight and insufficient reasons. The clause applies only to United States judges. They can grant the writ only in cases of violation of United States laws (see page 173).

4. Bill of Attainder.—*Attainder* in this phrase means that forfeiture of property and loss of all civil rights (among them, the right to inherit property or transmit it to heirs) which a person formerly suffered who had been condemned to death for treason or other crime. A *bill of attainder* is an act (i.e. a law) of a legislature inflicting this punishment upon some particular person and condemning him to death, without a regular trial in a court. Such laws are inconsistent with the principles of republican government, and are therefore properly prohibited to Congress **(46)**.

5. Ex post facto Law.—This is a law that makes punishable as a *crime* an act which was not criminal when done, or that increases the punishment of a crime after it has been committed.* Such laws are unjust, and therefore wholly forbidden to Congress **(46)**.

6. Direct Tax.—What a direct tax or capitation tax is has been already described (see Chap. XV., sec. 1 and 11). A prior clause has given the rule of apportionment of direct taxes **(5)**. For greater security it was provided that no direct tax should be laid except in that way, counting three-fifths of the slaves **(47)**. But now if direct taxes were laid they would be in proportion to true population.

7. Export Duties.—These are entirely forbidden to Congress **(48)**. The reasons have been given before (see page 135, sec. 5). This clause forms an exception to the one in sec. 8 **(26)** which gives the right to lay duties.

---

* If, for example, one should commit murder while the penalty was imprisonment for life, and the legislature should then pass a law, and apply it to his case, making the penalty death.

8. Equality in Trade.—It was the aim of the Constitution to secure to each State freedom and equality in trade. For this reason any preference of the ports of one State over those of another is forbidden **(48)**.*

9. Appropriations.—An *appropriation* is a law providing that a certain sum of money in the treasury shall be paid out for a certain purpose. The Constitution provides that no money shall be drawn out except when so appropriated by Congress **(49)**. This places the public money beyond the reach or control of the Executive or any other officer, and secures it in the hands of the representatives of the people. Even the President cannot draw his salary unless Congress makes the appropriation. In pursuance of this provision, Congress, at every session, passes laws specifying the objects for which money is to be appropriated.

10. Statements.—The clause requiring statements of the receipts and expenditures to be published makes Congress responsible to the people. Such statements are published annually, and short abstracts are published monthly **(49)**.

11. Titles of Nobility.†—Congress is entirely prohibited from granting these **(50)**. They would tend to introduce

---

* The last part of that clause, referring to entry, etc, may not be easily understood. It does not mean that vessels going from one State to another shall not be obliged to enter, clear or pay duties (as it might be literally construed). There are laws of Congress enforcing these things in certain cases. It means only that when a vessel is bound from a certain State it shall be obliged to clear only in that State, and when bound to a certain State it shall be obliged to enter or pay duties only in that State. The purpose was to prevent vessels from being compelled to enter, clear or pay duties at ports from which they did not come or to which they were not bound. This very hardship had been imposed upon American commerce before the Revolution by England, who compelled American vessels sailing to a foreign port to first go to England,

† See page 20, sec 6.

Legislative Department. 155

the distinctions of rank here that exist in many other countries, which the Constitution desires to prevent. As the Declaration of Independence says, "all men are created equal."

12. Relations of Officers with Foreign Sovereigns.—Officers of the United States Government are forbidden to receive any present, office, or title from any foreign state, unless with the consent of Congress **(50)**. This is to guard them against foreign influence.

CHAPTER XXXIII.

PROHIBITIONS ON THE STATES.

1. Treaties.—Section 10 of Article I. enumerates certain things which each State is forbidden to do. The first one is, to make any treaty, alliance, or confederation * **(51)**. Another clause forbids a State to make any kind of agreement with another State or with a foreign power without the consent of Congress **(52)**. If the States, separately, were allowed to make treaties or form alliances with foreign powers, the rights and interests of one State might be injured by the treaties made by another. As the States united constitute but one Nation, it is obvious that the power to treat with other nations properly belongs to the General Government.

2. Letters of Marque.—The States are forbidden to issue these, as by doing so one State might, for local reasons, direct the enmity of a foreign nation against the whole Nation, and perhaps involve the whole country in war.

---

* For the meaning of *treaty* see page 164. An *alliance* is a union for some common object. A *confederation* is a broader word, signifying a closer union.

3. Coinage.—This is forbidden to each State. One object in giving this power to Congress was that the coinage might be uniform (see page 143), but if each State had the power also, this object might not be attained.

4. Bills of Credit.—The States are forbidden to emit them. *Bills of credit* are promises to pay certain amounts of money, issued for the purpose of being used as money. The purpose of the clause was to prevent the future occurrence of the evils they had already caused.* The United States Treasury notes are bills of credit. Bank bills issued by state or national banks are not within the prohibition.

5. Legal Tender.—The States are forbidden to make anything but gold and silver coin a tender in payment of debts. Tender, or, as it is usually called, *legal tender*, means that with which a debt may be paid, by law.† Some of the States had declared their irredeemable paper money a lawful tender. But paper money and property of all kinds are continually liable to fluctuation in value, and might subject those who should be compelled to receive it to great inconvenience and loss. Gold and silver are considered more stable in their value.

6. Bill of Attainder.—This is forbidden to the state legislatures for the same reason that it is forbidden to Congress (see page 153, sec. 4).

7. Ex post facto Law.—The States are forbidden to pass such laws, as they are unjust (see page 153, sec. 5).

8. Law Impairing the Obligation of Contracts. — The

---

* *Bills of credit*, to a vast amount, were issued by the States during the Revolution, and for some time thereafter. This paper money, having no funds set apart to redeem it, became almost worthless.

† Not all money is legal tender. The legal tender in this country now is gold, silver, and U. S. notes (see page 143). The creditor may take what he chooses in payment of the debt, but he cannot be compelled to take anything but legal tender.

passage of such a law by any state legislature is forbidden. Laws that would release men from their obligations would be contrary to the principles of justice, and destroy all security for the rights of property.*

9. **Titles of Nobility.**—The granting of these by any State is forbidden, for the same reasons as in the case of Congress (see page 154, sec. 11).

10. **Duties.**—States are forbidden to lay duties on imports or exports (**52**). The reason that import duties are not allowed is that they may be uniform throughout the country. This has been explained before (page 135). Export duties are generally considered impolitic, as tending to discourage the industries of a country.

11. **Inspection Duties.**—The exception allowing a State to lay duties necessary to execute its inspection laws was deemed proper. Laws are passed by the States for the inspection or examination of flour and meat in barrels, leather, and sundry other commodities in commercial cities, to ascertain their quality and quantity, that they may be marked accordingly. By this means the States are enabled to improve the quality of articles produced by the labor of the country, and the articles are better fitted for sale, as the purchaser is therefore guarded against deception. A small tax is laid upon the goods inspected, to pay for their inspection. But, lest the States should carry this power so

---

* As bankrupt laws release debtors from the payment of their debts, and consequently impair the obligation of contracts, the question has arisen whether the States have power to pass them. From decisions of the Supreme Court of the United States, which is the highest judicial authority, it appears that a State may not pass a bankrupt law discharging a debtor from the obligation of a contract made before such law was passed. But it was not to be considered a law impairing the obligation of a contract, if it existed before the contract was made, because the parties, who are presumed to know that such l

far as to injure other States, these "laws are to be subject to the revision and control of Congress."

12. Tonnage Duties.—These are duties laid upon vessels; so much per ton.* They are forbidden to States (unless with the consent of Congress), as they are a means of regulating commerce, which is a subject given entirely to Congress.

13. War.—We have seen that war is another subject of which Congress is to have complete control (Ch. XXXI.). For this reason the States are forbidden to keep troops or ships of war in time of peace, or to engage in war, without the consent of Congress.

PROHIBITIONS.

[In Art. I. sec. 9 and 10.]

I. ON THE UNITED STATES.

I. On Congress; as to
- I. Taxes;
  1. Export Duties,
  2. Direct taxes, not in proportion to census.
- II. Commerce;
  1. Abolition of Slave-Trade prior to 1808,
  2. Preference of Ports.
- III. Other Laws;
  1. Suspension of Habeas Corpus,
  2. Bill of Attainder,
  3. Ex post facto Law,
  4. Title of Nobility.

II. On U. S. Officers;
1. Paying Money without Appropriation,
2. Receiving from Foreign State, any
   1. Present,
   2. Emolument,
   3. Office, or
   4. Title.

---

* A vessel's tonnage is not what she weighs, but the number of tons of freight she can carry.

II. **ON THE STATES**; AS TO

   I. **Taxes;**
      1. Import Duties,
      2. Export Duties,
      3. Tonnage Duties.

   II. **Agreements with other States or Nations;**
      1. Treaty, etc.,
      2. Any Agreement.

   III. **War;**
      1. Letters of Marque,
      2. Troops, or War-vessels,
      3. Engaging in War.

   IV. **Money;**
      1. Coinage,
      2. Bills of Credit,
      3. Legal Tender.

   V. **Other Laws;**
      1. Bill of Attainder,
      2. Ex post facto Law,
      3. Law impairing Contract,
      4. Title of Nobility.

SECTION III.

EXECUTIVE DEPARTMENT.

CHAPTER XXXIV.

PRESIDENT AND VICE-PRESIDENT: ELECTION, QUALIFICATIONS, ETC.

1. Executive.—One of the strongest distinctions between the present Union and the Confederation is that now we have a full and strong executive department, while under the Confederation there was none (see page 94).

2. Number.—In regard to the organization and powers of the executive department there was great diversity of opinion in the Constitutional Convention. The three principal points discussed were (1) whether it should consist of one person as chief, or more, (2) the term, and (3) the mode of election. First: ought the chief executive power to be vested in one person, or a number of persons? Laws should be executed with promptness and energy. This is more likely to be done by one man than by a number. If several were associated in the exercise of this power, disagreement and discord would be likely to happen, and to cause frequent and injurious delays. For this reason it was decided to have one President (**53**).

3. Term.—Second: as to the term. It was argued that the term should not be so short as to induce him to act more with a view to his re-election than to the public good, nor so short that he would not feel some independence of the people, and could not carry out his system of public policy; nor so long that he would feel too independent of the people. The term of four years was decided upon as the most likely to avoid all the objections (**53**). It commences March 4th next after the election.* A new Congress is elected and begins its term at the same time as each successive Presidential term.

4. Mode of Election.—Third: as to the manner of electing the President. Several modes were proposed in the Convention, among them these: by Congress, by the state legislatures, by the people directly, and by Electors chosen for the purpose in some way. The last was the one adopted (**54**). The object was twofold: (1) to keep the legislative and executive departments distinct,† and (2) to make certain of such a man being elected as would be worthy of the high position. If Congress elected him, it would be practically combining the two departments; and on the other hand, if the people elected him directly, it was thought that they might be led into error through popular enthusiasm or misconception, and that at the time of an election there would be great excitement; but if he was elected by a body of select men, they would act with more deliberation and their judgment would be probably correct. And if they were selected for that one purpose it was thought they would be better fitted for it than the state legislatures would be.

5. Election of Electors.—The Constitution does not prescribe the manner in which the Electors shall be appointed or chosen; this is left to the States. At first no uniform mode was adopted by the different States, but at present in all the States they are selected directly by the people,

---

* The next election now (1880) occurs this year, and the next term commences March 4th, 1881.

† For this reason no Member of Congress nor civil officer can be an Elector.

usually, by *general ticket*.* By a law of Congress, the Electors are required to be chosen in all the States on the same day, which is the Tuesday next after the first Monday of November.

6. **Proceedings of Electors.**—On the first Wednesday of December the Electors meet in their respective States and vote for President and Vice-President. What follows is amply described in the Constitution itself (Amend. XII.). In 1804 a change was made in the mode of electing the Vice-President.†

7. **Election by the House.**—On the second Wednesday in February after the election the Electoral votes are counted, and if no one has obtained a majority, the House and Senate elect the President and Vice-President respectively. This is described in the Constitution and need not be repeated here (**95**).‡

8. **Present Practice.**—When the Constitution was framed it was intended that the Presidential Electors should exercise their own personal judgment, and that thus the President should be selected by the calm wisdom of a body of men selected for their fitness to perform such a duty. But the existence of political parties and their action has nullified the plan. Now the nominating conventions put forward the candidates for the Presidency, and the Electors are afterwards nominated and voted for entirely with reference to those candidates, it being known beforehand which one of the candidates they will vote for; and they never exercise their judgment, but simply record the vote of the people. It is unfortunate that the original plan could not

---

* That is, every voter votes for as many men as the State is entitled to have Electors.

† The Constitution itself shows what this was (55, 95).

‡ The President has been elected by the House twice; Jefferson in 1801, and John Quincy Adams in 1825.

have succeeded, for the present practice is open to the objections of an election directly by the people, which it is in effect.

9. Qualifications.—These the Constitution specifies (**57**). It will be noted that they are higher than those required for a Senator, because the office is so much more important. No length of residence here by a foreigner will qualify him.

10. Vacancy.—In case of a vacancy in the office of President, the Vice-President becomes the President.* Under the provision of the Constitution which allows it (**58**), Congress has enacted that, when there is neither President nor Vice-President, the President *pro tempore* of the Senate shall act as President; and if there should be none, the Speaker of the House of Representatives.

11. Salary.—The President has a salary, its amount being fixed by Congress.† Congress may increase or diminish it, but not so as to affect the President in office at the time (**59**). If Congress could reduce his salary at pleasure he could never afford to be independent of them. On the other hand, if it could be increased during his official term, he might be tempted to use undue influence to procure a needless increase.

CHAPTER XXXV.

POWERS AND DUTIES OF THE PRESIDENT.

1. Commander-in-Chief.—The President is commander-in-chief of the entire military force of the Nation (**61**).

---

* The Vice-President has no duties to perform as Executive of the Nation. He merely presides in the Senate. In dignity the office of President is much higher.

† Now (1880) $50,000 a year.

This power must be given into the hands of one man. If there were more (even two) there might be no firmness or promptitude, qualities absolutely necessary to render any army useful. The President is the proper person, for he is the Executive of the Nation. But the President does not take the field himself. The actual operations are conducted by his generals under his supervision.

2. **Reprieves and Pardons.***—These may be granted by the President, but only in cases of convictions by the United States courts **(61)**. Over state offences he has no jurisdiction. Peculiar cases may arise where, although a person is adjudged guilty of a crime, he does not deserve the punishment the law provides; as if, for instance, new evidence should arise showing him to be innocent. But the pardoning power may be greatly abused, and some claim that it would be better to take it away altogether.

3. **Treaties.**—A *treaty* is an agreement between nations, and it may be upon any subject: for peace, for war against some third power, concerning commerce, the mail, the return of escaped criminals, or any other subject. The power to make them for the United States rests with the President. But this is so important a duty that it is not entrusted to him alone, but two-thirds of the Senate must concur **(62)**.†

4. **Ministers.**—These are officers sent to a foreign nation to represent their own nation there. In this country they are appointed by the President, with the advice and

---

* See page 46, sec. 7.

† Treaties are *negotiated;* that is, the provisions or terms are arranged and agreed upon, by the agents of the two governments; and a copy of the articles of agreement is sent to each government to be *ratified*. Both governments must ratify, or the treaty fails. Treaties are ratified, on the part of our government, by the President and Senate. This is what is meant by their making treaties.

consent of the Senate. They are often called *ambassadors*. Our government sends a minister to each of the civilized and semi-civilized nations of the world. They reside abroad and transact any business that our government may have with the government of the country where they are. They often negotiate treaties.*

5. Consuls.—These the President appoints in the same way. *Consuls* are agents of inferior grade. They reside in foreign seaports. Their business is to aid their respective governments in their commercial transactions with the countries in which they reside, and to protect the rights, commerce, merchants, and seamen of their own nation. Hence much of their business is with masters of vessels and with merchants.

6. Judges.—The President and Senate appoint also the judges of the Supreme Court, and of the Circuit and District courts.

7. Other Appointments.—Thus we see that the President has very important powers of appointment. Nor is he under the control of the Senate always, for under the Constitution **(62)** Congress has vested the appointment of very many inferior officers in him alone, or in the Heads of Departments, who are appointed by him and more or less under his influence. The advantage is that a President is thus better able to carry out his own policy if he has the selection of those who shall aid him. But the danger is

---

* Strictly our country has never sent ambassadors, but *ministers plenipotentiary*. An ambassador who is intrusted with the ordinary business of a minister at a foreign court, and who lives there, is called an *ambassador in ordinary*. An *ambassador extraordinary* is a person sent on a particular occasion, who returns as soon as the business on which he was sent is done. He is sometimes called *envoy;* and when he has power to act as he may deem expedient, he is called *envoy plenipotentiary;* the latter word signifying full power.

that if we should obtain an ambitious or unprincipled President he might use the power of appointment simply to reward those who would advance his own interests, and greatly to the injury of the people.*

8. Vacancies.—But in those cases where the Senate must concur in appointments, vacancies will often occur while the Senate is not in session. In such cases the President may alone make temporary appointments (**63**). Without such a power somewhere, the public interests would often suffer serious injury. When the Senate acts on appointments it is said to go into *executive session.*

9. Removals.—Most of the officers, clerks, etc., in the Civil Service † of the United States are appointed for no particular term, but hold office until the appointing authority removes them. Those appointed by the President, or any other officer alone, can be removed by him or such officer at any time. With regard to those whose appointments the Senate must concur in, it was urged at first by many that the consent of the Senate must also be obtained to the removal, but this has not been the practice. Up to 1867 the President exercised the power of removal alone in all cases. In that year the "tenure of office act"

---

* For some time past the two political parties have used this power to advance their own interests, and when a new party has come into power very many of the civil officers have been removed without cause in order that members of that party might be appointed in their stead. The aim of Civil Service Reform is to establish the custom of retaining officers, at least of inferior rank, as long as they do their duty, and of appointing those best fitted for the office, no matter to which party they belong. This is the policy of England, and ought to be of our country.

† The "Civil Service" means the body of persons employed by the United States, from the Cabinet down to the lowest clerks in the Post-Office, except the army and navy. It includes now perhaps 100,000 persons.

was passed, requiring the consent of the Senate to the removal of those officers whose appointment they must concur in.

10. Message.—At every session the President sends to Congress a *message*, containing recommendations of the passage of such measures as he judges expedient (**64**). This, of course, gives little information, but it serves to fix the responsibility upon them.

11. Convening Congress.—Besides the regular sessions each year, Congress may be convened by the President when he thinks an extraordinary occasion has arisen such as to render it necessary, but at such times they only act upon the subjects he lays before them.

12. Reception of Foreign Ministers.—This is devolved upon the President as the proper person to represent the Nation. It is usually a merely formal matter, but may be one of great importance. In case a revolution has occurred in some foreign country and a new minister is sent here, the President in deciding whom he will receive must decide whether to recognize the new or the old government, and this might involve us in war.

13. Execution of the Laws.—This is the most important and most comprehensive duty devolved upon the President. It calls upon him to see that above all things obedience is rendered to all the laws of the Union. It is for this purpose that he is made commander of the army and navy. In 1861 President Lincoln would have disregarded this high obligation had he refused to take every means to subdue those States which had openly revolted from the authority of the Nation.

By comparing this chapter with Chapter XI. it will be seen how similar the powers and duties of the President are to those of a state governor; but those of the former are as much more important in their exercise than those of the latter, as the Nation is greater than any State. The state constitutions generally have been modelled on the United States Constitution.

CHAPTER XXXVI.

AUXILIARY EXECUTIVE DEPARTMENTS.

1. Departments.—The great amount and variety of the executive business of the Nation require the division of the executive department into several subordinate departments, and the distribution among them of the different kinds of public business. These departments are seven in number, named as follows: (1) Department of State, (2) Department of the Treasury, (3) Department of the Interior, (4) Department of War, (5) Department of the Navy, (6) Department of Justice, and (7) Post-Office Department.

2. Cabinet.—At the head of each of these Departments is a chief officer. These chief officers, sometimes called *Heads of Departments*, are named respectively the Secretaries of State, of the Treasury, of the Interior, of War, and of the Navy, the Attorney-General and Postmaster-General, and are appointed by the President with the consent of the Senate. Together they form a sort of council and act as advisers of the President. As such they are called the *Cabinet*. Owing to this close relation between a President and his Cabinet it is usual for the Senate to confirm whomever the President selects for cabinet officers.*

3. Department of State.—This department has charge of all the business of the Nation with foreign nations. The

---

* There is also a Department of Agriculture, but its chief officer, the Commissioner of Agriculture, is not a Cabinet officer.

Secretary of State conducts all our diplomatic * correspondence, being the official organ of communication with the ministers of foreign governments sent to this country, and with our ministers abroad. He is also the custodian of the seal, the laws, and other official documents of the Nation.

4. Department of the Treasury.—To this belongs the charge of the finances of the Nation. It collects the revenue from customs and excises, pays the debts of the Nation, coins the money, and takes charge of all money paid to the government. The vast amount of business in this department requires a great number of assistants. All the custom-houses, mints, and sub-treasuries form part of it. The building devoted to its business in Washington is one of the largest there.

5. Department of the Interior.—The chief subjects of which this department has charge are the taking of the *census* every ten years (5), the management and sale of the *public lands*, the management of the *Indians*, the payment of *pensions*,† and the granting of *patents*.

6. Department of War.—This department has charge of the procuring of supplies and equipment and other matters relating to the army. Its duties are of course far more important in time of war than in peace. The coast signal service belongs to this department.

7. Department of the Navy.—This department has charge of the navy, the procuring of supplies and equipment of vessels of war, etc.

---

* *Diplomacy* is the science of conducting negotiations between nations.

† A *pension* is a yearly allowance to a person by the government for past services. In this country pensions are granted to those who are disabled in war. If a soldier is killed a pension is granted to his widow or children. The amount of pensions now paid in this country is very large, amounting to about $30,000,000 yearly.

8. Department of Justice.—The duties of the Attorney-General and his assistants are to attend to all suits in the United States courts in which the United States is interested, and to give their opinions in writing on legal questions when requested by the President or Heads of Departments.

9. Post-Office Department.—This has charge of the mail. All post-offices form a part of it. The Postmaster-General establishes post-offices, provides for carrying the mail, and has general charge of all matters connected with it.

10. Reports.—Each of the Departments makes an annual report to Congress of the business transacted therein during the year. These are published. Thus the people are kept informed of what is done, and valuable statistics are collected with regard to the receipts, expenditures, and debt of the Nation, the exports and imports, etc.

SECTION IV.

JUDICIAL DEPARTMENT.

CHAPTER XXXVII.

NATIONAL COURTS AND THEIR JURISDICTION.

a. Courts.

1. Necessity for National Judiciary.—We now come to the third article of the Constitution, providing a national judicial department. The Confederation had none, and was thus dependent on the States. The chief reason why a national judiciary is necessary in addition to the state systems is that the state judges might be biased in favor of their own State. Laws of Congress often bear with greater hardship on some States than on others, and public opinion in those States upon whom the burden lay might be so strong in opposition that no judge elected and supported by those people would sustain it. But if the judge belonged to a national system, and thus represented and was supported by the whole Nation, he would have nothing to fear and thus his decision would be more impartial. The experience of the Confederation taught this.

2. Courts.—The national judiciary system consists of three grades of courts: the *Supreme Court*, the *Circuit Courts*, and the *District Courts*. The Supreme Court is the highest court in the land, and was established by the Constitution itself **(66)**. The others were established by

Congress. The Supreme Court consists of nine judges, and its jurisdiction is almost wholly appellate; that is, cases are not tried in it, but it only hears appeals from the other courts, and that only in the most important cases. It has original jurisdiction in a few cases. Of the Circuit Courts there are nine in the country. They are next lower in grade to the Supreme Court, to which appeals are taken from them. There are fifty-eight District Courts, and they are the lowest in grade. They hear the smaller cases, and appeals are taken from them to the Circuit Courts. The jurisdiction of all the courts is both civil and criminal.*

3. **Court of Claims.**—No one has any right to sue a government. Such a right is inconsistent with sovereignty. So, in this country, no one has a right to sue the people (they are the government), for it is the people from whom he gets any right, even the right to his own property or his life, and to admit that any one had a right to force anything from them would be admitting that they were not sovereign. For this reason no one has a right to sue the United States, or any State (94). But Congress has established a court called the *Court of Claims*, in which those having claims which they think ought to be paid by the United States may bring a suit in the ordinary way, in form against the United States, and the court decides whether they should be paid. If it is decided in the claimant's favor it is so reported to Congress, and Congress generally will make an appropriation. But Congress is free to do as it chooses, and there is no way to compel payment. Some States have established similar courts of claims, but though proceeding in legal methods, they perform rather the functions of legislative committees than courts.

4. **Tenure of Office.**—By the Constitution the judges

---

* For explanation of the terms used in this section see page 76.

hold office during good behavior **(66)**. This means until removed on impeachment for bad behavior, and thus in most cases it means for life. In no other department of the general government are offices held for so long a term. The purpose is to insure a correct and impartial administration of justice by making them independent. If they could be displaced at the pleasure of the appointing power, or by frequent elections, they might be tempted to conform their opinions and decisions to the wishes of those on whom they were dependent for continuance in office. The object of the framers of the Constitution was to remove them as far as possible from party influence.

5. Salary.—As with the President, so here, Congress, though it fixes the salaries of the judges, cannot diminish them while in office. To give Congress power over the purse of an officer is to give it power over his will. Dependence upon the legislature would be as great an evil as dependence upon the appointing power.

b. Jurisdiction.

6. In General.—The jurisdiction of the United States courts does not extend to all kinds of cases, but only to such as the Constitution specifies, just as Congress has power to pass only such laws as the Constitution allows it to. The cases enumerated in the Constitution **(67)** in which the national courts have jurisdiction may be divided into three general classes, (1) those arising under the Constitution, the laws of Congress, and treaties, (2) those affecting foreigners, and (3) those between different States or the citizens of different States.*

---

* It will be seen, therefore, that the great majority of cases between citizens of the same State must be brought in the state courts. So also the great majority of criminal cases are tried in the state courts.

7. Cases arising under United States Laws.—Cases which arise under the Constitution, laws, or treaties of the United States may be those where a person is given a right by the Constitution, laws, or treaties which he does not have by the laws of his State (as, for instance, a right to sue an infringer of a patent granted to him), or where he violates a law of Congress or treaty (as counterfeiting coin, or doing anything forbidden by a treaty), or where any question arises as to the meaning of the Constitution, laws, or treaties of the United States, or as to whether a law of Congress is constitutional * or not. In these cases it makes no difference whether the parties are citizens of the same State or not. The jurisdiction is given to the national judiciary for two reasons: (1) in order that in the interpretation and enforcement of its own laws it may not be dependent on the States, and (2) in order that the interpretation may be uniform throughout the country. Were it left to the state courts some States might decide that a law meant one thing and other States that it meant another.

8. Cases affecting Foreigners.—The decision of these properly belongs to the national courts, for the reason that if a foreigner is injured here, the Nation, and not the State, is responsible to the foreigner's government: therefore the Nation, and not the State, should redress the injury. And where the foreigner is an ambassador, or other minister, the Supreme Court has original jurisdiction of the case (68). This is in order to provide as certainly as possible

---

* A law of Congress is unconstitutional (and wholly void) unless the Constitution has given Congress the right to pass it (see page 133). If, for instance, Congress should pass a usury law (that is, a law regulating the interest of money), or a law abolishing capital punishment, it would be void, because it has not been given these powers by the Constitution.

against the danger of injustice being done, for it might involve the country in a dispute, or even war, with his country. All public ministers are treated with the highest respect, for this reason. Admiralty jurisdiction* is also given to the national courts, for the reason that many admiralty cases affect foreigners. Another reason is that admiralty is a part of the regulation of commerce, which we have seen is a subject taken away from the States and given entirely to the United States.

9. Cases affecting different States, or their Citizens.— The third class of cases in which the national courts have jurisdiction is where the parties on the two sides, plaintiff and defendant, are either two different States, or citizens of different States. The reason for this jurisdiction is to prevent dissension among the States. If the decision of a question which affected two States were left to the courts of either, the controversy instead of being closed would be intensified. The history of the small German States and of the States under the Confederation illustrates this. But now, there being an impartial arbiter, the United States, the States submit to the decision.†

---

* Admiralty jurisdiction is jurisdiction of cases arising on the sea, or connected with vessels; as, for instance, cases of piracy, of collision on the sea, or claims for repairing a vessel, or contracts to carry freight or passengers. No State has any jurisdiction over the ocean.

† It will be noticed that the jurisdiction in the cases mentioned in this and the preceding section depends upon the character of the persons suing or sued, while in those mentioned in section 7 it depends upon the character of the case. When the case is such as to give the national courts jurisdiction it makes no difference whether the parties are citizens of different States or not, and when they are citizens of different States, or one is a foreigner, those courts have jurisdiction whether the case is one of those mentioned in section 7 or not. Not all the cases enumerated in sec. 2 of Art. III (67) have

CHAPTER XXXVIII.

TREASON.

1. Why Defined.—Treason is one of the highest crimes that man can commit. Yet, such deep resentment and alarm does it create among the people, for it is an attempt to overthrow the established government, that the tendency always is to see it in acts which may be innocent, and which at least do not have such a purpose. For this reason the Constitution itself says what shall be considered treason, and what proof shall be necessary to establish it **(70)**. It must be either making war against the Nation, or adhering to its enemies. And it is not sufficient that there is an intention or even a conspiracy to do these things, though they are highly reprehensible. There must be some overt (i.e. open) act, before it is treason.

2. Proof.—The proof required is more than in the case of most crimes. Generally one may be convicted, even of murder, upon the testimony of one witness directly to the commission of the crime, or even without any direct testimony upon its commission, provided the other circumstances proven point toward it. But in treason against the United States, no matter what circumstances point toward it, there must be two witnesses to the same act.

3. Punishment.—Under the authority given by the Con-

---

been spoken of separately in the text. It will be a useful exercise for the pupil to write down each separate case mentioned there, and tell to which one of the three classes described above it belongs, and why. But he will be apt to make a mistake as to suits by citizens against States, unless he consults Amendment XI. (see page 188). A State cannot be sued except by another State,

stitution (**71**) Congress has declared the punishment of treason to be death, or, at the discretion of the court, imprisonment and fine; the imprisonment to be for not less than five years and the fine not less than $10,000. An *attainder* of treason means here judgment by a court. In England formerly, when one was adjudged guilty of treason all his property was forfeited to the king, and he could neither inherit nor transmit property to heirs. This is what is meant by *corruption of blood.* Thus for a man's treason his innocent relatives were punished with him. But that is not so here. A law of Congress provides that no conviction (of any crime against the United States) shall work corruption of blood or any forfeiture of estate.

4. The Civil War.—In this country there were no prosecutions for treason after the War, even of the leaders. They were, however, laid under certain political disabilities, but even these have now (1880) been almost entirely removed.

5. Other Crimes.—The great majority of crimes, such as murder, forgery, theft, etc., lie generally within the jurisdiction of the State. The state laws describe them, and the state courts punish them. The other subjects, beside treason, upon which Congress has authority to define offences and establish their punishment, and of which the national courts have criminal jurisdiction, are chiefly as follows: *All* crimes committed on the *sea,* piracy, murder, theft, etc.; *perjury* and other judicial crimes when committed *in the national courts; counterfeiting* United States notes or coin; *forgery* of patents or other *United States papers;* robbery of the *mail,* or other crimes connected with the postal service; *extortion* by a *United States officer;* the holding of *slaves;* and preventing any one from exercising his civil rights, by *intimidation* or other means.

SECTION V.

MISCELLANEOUS PROVISIONS.

CHAPTER XXXIX.

RELATIONS OF STATES.

1. Records.—Article IV. of the Constitution contains a number of important provisions, most of which affect the relations of the States to each other and to the General Government. The first one is in regard to the effect which the laws, records, and judgments of one State shall have in another, and the provision is that they shall have full effect everywhere **(72)**. For instance, if a person is sued in New York and there is a decision on the merits against him, it is decided once for all, and it may be enforced against him wherever he goes. Were it not for this clause States might provide that no matter how many times a question had been tried, it must be tried over again with all the evidence before they would enforce it. Congress has prescribed the manner in which public acts and records may be proved, and when proven they are conclusive as to the things stated in them.

2. Privileges of Citizens.—No State can grant privileges to its own citizens, from which the citizens of other States are excluded **(73)**. The purpose is to put all on an equality everywhere. Without such a provision, any State might deny to citizens of other States, the right to buy and hold real estate, or to become voters after living in the State the prescribed time, or to enjoy equal privileges in trade or business.

3. Fugitive Criminals.—The officials of one State have no power in another State as officials. For instance, the police or sheriff of New York City have no power to arrest a murderer in Jersey City. But the Constitution provides against the escape of criminals in this way **(74)**. The Governor of the State from which such person has fled, sends a *requisition* to the Governor of the State in which he is found, demanding his delivery to the first State. This requisition is usually complied with, and yet cases have occurred in which a Governor has refused to deliver up an accused person, and there is no way provided to compel him. This seems to have been an oversight on the part of the framers of the Constitution.

4. Fugitive Slaves.—By the common law, a slave escaping into a non-slaveholding State became free. As it was presumed at the time the Constitution was framed that other Northern States would follow Massachusetts in abolishing slavery, the Southern States wanted some provision to enable them to reclaim their fugitive slaves. The Northern States, though opposed to this, yielded for the sake of unity **(75)**. Escaped slaves were, under this provision, returned to the South up to 1861. The clause is of course obsolete now.*

5. New States.—The provision **(76)** with regard to the admission of new States into the Union was deemed necessary in view of the large extent of vacant lands within the United States, and of the inconvenient size of some of the States then existing. The territory north-west of the Ohio

---

* The word "slave" does not appear in the original Constitution. The framers knew that it would be a blot upon the Constitution of a *free* country.

River had been ceded to the General Government by the States claiming the same. South of the Ohio River also was a large tract, principally unsettled, within the chartered limits of Virginia, North Carolina, and Georgia, extending west to the Mississippi. These two tracts it was presumed would soon become so thickly populated as to require separate governments. Since that time vast tracts have been acquired from France, Spain, Texas, and Mexico. From all these tracts twenty-five new States have been formed and admitted into the Union. When formed from the territory of the United States the consent of Congress only is required, but when formed from the territory of another State the consent of that State must also be obtained.*

6. United States Territory.—Congress has complete power over the territory not organized into States (**77**). It establishes territorial governments, and these carry on all the ordinary governmental duties, but they are subject to the control of Congress. The clause with regard to the claims of States has no effect at the present day.

7. Protection by United States.—The United States must always see to it that the state governments are republican in form (**78**). The object is to perpetuate republican institutions. If some large State should establish a monarchy, it might in time engulf smaller ones, and in the end destroy the Constitution. Its policy would be in opposition to all republican institutions. So, if a State is in danger from invasion, or insurrection, it may call on the Nation for assistance.

---

* After the late war Congress declared the Southern States to have no lawful governments, and placed them under temporary military governments. In time they adopted new constitutions, and were re-admitted to the Union by Congress.

CHAPTER XL.

AMENDMENT: DEBT: SUPREMACY: OATH: TEST: RATIFICATION.

1. Reason for Amendment.—Article V. describes the manner in which the Constitution may be amended (**79**). As the best human government is imperfect, and as all the future wants and necessities of a people cannot be foreseen and provided for, it is obvious that every constitution should contain some provision for its amendment.

2. Mode of Amendment.—This is described in the Constitution (**79**). If amendments could be made whenever desired by a bare majority of the States, the strength and efficiency of the Constitution might be greatly impaired by frequent alterations. It is therefore wisely provided that a mere proposition to amend cannot be made except by a majority of at least two-thirds of Congress, or of the legislatures of at least two-thirds of the States; and that such proposition must be ratified by a still larger majority (three-fourths) of the States. It was thought better to submit occasionally to some temporary inconvenience than to indulge in frequent amendments..

3. Public Debt.—The clause (**80**) which adopts the prior debts of the country was intended to allay the fears of public creditors, who apprehended that a change in the government would release the Nation from its obligations. But their fears were probably groundless, for one purpose in changing the government was to provide a way to pay those debts.

4. Supremacy.—The next clause (**81**) declares that the Constitution, the treaties and the laws of Congress shall prevail over any state law or constitution. This is the clause giving efficacy to the whole Constitution. If any State could nullify the national law, nothing would be gained by the Union. Now, when a state law or state constitution is passed contrary to the law of the Nation every one must consider it void, and the state judges must declare it so.

5. **Oath of Allegiance.**—All members of all state and national, legislative, executive, and judicial departments are required on taking office to take the oath of allegiance, i.e. to support the Constitution of the United States **(82)**. Binding the conscience of public officers by oath or solemn affirmation has ever been considered necessary to secure a faithful performance of their duties. They are generally required to swear not only to support the Constitution, but also to discharge the duties of their offices to the best of their ability.

6. **Test Oath.**—In the same clause, *test* (often called *test oath*) means an oath or a declaration in favor of or against certain religious opinions, as a qualification for office. In England, all officers, civil and military, were formerly obliged to make a declaration against transubstantiation, and to assent to the doctrines and conform to the rules of the established church. The object of forbidding it here was to secure to every citizen the full enjoyment of religious liberty. But this clause does not bind the States. They can provide tests, but usually they have similar clauses in their constitutions.

7. **Ratification.**—By the Constitution **(83)** nine States were to ratify it before it had binding effect in any. The immediate ratification of the Constitution by all the States was hardly to be expected; a unanimous ratification, therefore, was not required. But a Union of less than nine States was deemed inexpedient. The framers concluded their labors on the 17th of September, 1787; and in July,

1788, the ratification of New Hampshire, the ninth State, was received by Congress.*

8. Commencement of Government.—Thus in July, 1788, the government had begun. During 1788 and the early part of 1789, Senators, Representatives, and Presidential Electors were chosen by the States. In February, 1789, General Washington was elected President by the Electors, and was inaugurated April 30th following, when the 1st Constitutional Congress assembled. Thus we see that our government is not yet a century old.

CHAPTER XLI.

THE FIRST TWELVE AMENDMENTS.

1. In General.—It is remarkable that during so long a period the Constitution has received so few changes. Up to 1865, though twelve amendments had been added, only the last two of them had made any alteration in the original provisions. This proves the wisdom and skill of the patriots who framed it, to whom we should be ever duly grateful for having furnished our country with so admirable a bulwark of liberty.

2. Bill of Rights.—This is a name given to the first ten amendments, because they contain a list of the rights

---

* The Constitution could not become binding on any State except by its own ratification, for the State was sovereign. But with amendments it is different. When accepted by three-fourths they are binding on all. They have given up their sovereignty to this extent By accepting the Constitution at first each State agreed that amendments might be made binding in that way, even against their consent.

deemed most important to the liberty of the people. These amendments do not change any original provision of the Constitution. They act merely as restrictions and limitations upon the powers of Congress, and were deemed unnecessary by those who framed the Constitution, for the reason that those rights were so generally acknowledged, and that the powers of Congress were limited to those expressly granted to it. But as several of the state conventions had, at the time of adopting the Constitution, expressed a desire that declarations and guaranties of certain rights should be added, in order to prevent misconstruction and abuse, the first Congress, at its first session, proposed twelve amendments, ten of which were ratified by the requisite number of States.

3. Its Purpose.—As long as popular liberty lasted sufficient to maintain any part of the Constitution it is not probable that any of these rights would have been violated, even had they remained unexpressed. And yet it was of value to express them. They are thus kept in the mind of all, serving as reminders, both to the ambitious man who in his power grows neglectful of the people's rights, and to the people themselves, who sometimes, through excitement and sudden indignation, are inclined to forget the rights they have guaranteed to every one. It is important to remember that the first twelve amendments affect only Congress and the national courts, not the state legislatures. For this reason similar provisions are often inserted in state constitutions, to bind the state legislatures and courts. We will refer briefly to these amendments in their order.

4. Religious Freedom.—The object of the 1st Amendment was to prevent the National Government from abridging religious freedom in any degree (**84, 82**). In England, though all were free to worship as they chose, yet there was an established church, supported by the government. Here it was thought best not only to have perfect liberty in religion, but also to have the Church and State entirely separate.

5. Freedom of Speech and of the Press.—These have been before defined (page 16). Congress is forbidden to pass any law abridging them **(84)**. The object of this provision was not to allow one to go unpunished who uttered slander or published libel. It was intended to prevent all use of those means which in former times had been used to repress the people, by forbidding them to speak or write on certain subjects unless licensed by the government beforehand. At one time it was the law in certain countries that even the Bible should not be printed except in a certain language, which the people did not understand. So, also, governments would require all books to be licensed before they could be printed, and would forbid the utterance of any criticism, no matter how just or honest, against them or their officers.

6. Right to Assemble.—So, too, Congress is forbidden to pass any law abridging the right of the people to assemble and present petitions to the government **(84)**. Under pretense of preventing insurrection governments have at times denied the people this right.

7. Right to Keep Arms.—This means the right of every one to own and use, in a peaceful manner, warlike weapons; Congress is forbidden to pass any law infringing the right **(85)**. It was thought that without it, ambitious men might, by the aid of the regular army, overthrow the liberties of the people and usurp the powers of government.

8. Quartering of Soldiers in Private Houses.—The 3d Amendment arose from a remembrance of past experience **(86)**. Among the grievances enumerated in the Declaration of Independence was one "for quartering large bodies of armed troops" among the people of the Colonies.

9. Searches and Seizures.—A *search-warrant* is a paper issued by a court directing a person's premises to be searched, because it is suspected there is stolen property there or property subject to duty. A *seizure* is the taking of such property, or the arrest of the person, by the officer. In the early times of English history these had been converted into instruments of tyranny. Search-warrants had been sometimes granted when no accusation had been made, and in blank, so that by filling out the blank the officer could search any house he chose. The 4th Amendment forbids Congress to pass any law authorizing warrants to issue, except when good cause is shown, and supported by oath (**87**).

10. Criminal Proceedings.—The object of most of the provisions of the 5th and 6th Amendments is the protection of one accused of crime. Popular opinion is generally hasty in cases of crime, and the rights named in these amendments, most of which are easily understood,* are such as had been found necessary in the history of justice in England to save innocent persons from punishment. By them Congress is forbidden to pass any law infringing these rights (**88, 89**). So important was the trial by jury in criminal cases considered that it had been inserted in the body of the Constitution (**69**).

11. Private Property.—Every government of unlimited powers has the right to take the private property of any person, for some public use, and it may be done even without compensation. This is called the right of *eminent domain*. But even in those cases where Congress has this right, the 5th Amendment forbids its exercise without just compensation being paid the private owner (**88**).

---

* In the 5th Amendment "twice put in jeopardy" means tried again after having been once acquitted.

12. Trial by Jury in Civil Cases.—We have seen that the jury trial is secured in criminal cases **(69)**. The 7th Amendment requires it in civil cases * also **(90)**. Both these provisions refer only to cases in United States courts. The 7th Amendment also provides what the effect of a jury's verdict shall be. By the rules of the common law when a jury had rendered a decision upon a question of fact upon which some witnesses had testified in one way and others in another, that question could not be re-examined in a higher court. After the passage of the Constitution it was thought that the clause which gives the Supreme Court appellate jurisdiction both as to law *and fact* **(68)** might give it power to overthrow the verdict of a jury, and therefore this amendment was added. Thus we see how carefully the Constitution protects the security, liberty, and property of the people.

13. Excessive Bail.—Bail has been described (page 84). But it will be seen that the amount of the bond might be fixed so high as to prevent persons accused of crime from procuring the necessary sureties; whereby innocent persons might be subjected to long imprisonment before the time of trial. To prevent this in the United States courts is the object of the 8th Amendment. So, also, the degree of punishment is often left to the discretion of the court, as in the case of treason, where any amount of fine over $10,000 may be imposed. This amendment serves as a safeguard against excess **(91)**.

14. Rights of People.—There were those who feared that, because the Constitution mentioned certain rights as belonging to the people, those not mentioned might be

---

* The amendment says "suits at common law." These are distinguished from suits in *equity* or *admiralty*. It is unnecessary to give the meanings of these terms here. "Common-law suits" include a large majority of all civil cases.

considered as having been surrendered to the General Government, or as having never existed. To prevent such possible misconstruction was the object of the 9th Amendment (**92**).

15. Powers not Delegated.—So, also, the 10th Amendment was strictly unnecessary, for it is self-evident that what one has and does not give away he still retains (see page 133). But many were fearful that the central government might absorb the powers rightfully belonging to the States, and this was inserted to prevent such abuse (**93**).

16. Suits against States.—No state court can entertain any suit against a State. The 11th Amendment forbids the United States courts to entertain them (except by one State against another) (**94**). During the Revolution the States had issued bills of credit which had not been paid. After the adoption of the Constitution suits were brought against some of the States by private persons to enforce payment of these bills of credit, and the Supreme Court decided that under the judicial clause (**67**) this could be done. It was in consequence of this decision that the amendment was passed. Now there is no way for a private person to sue a State in any court. It is thought best to leave a State free to settle its obligations in its own way and in its own time.

17. Election of President.—This is the subject of the 12th Amendment (**95, 96**), and has been elsewhere treated (page 160). This amendment was adopted in 1804. Under the plan first adopted the chief opponent of the President became the Vice-President, and as the country had become divided into two great opposing parties, they would naturally belong each to one of those. Now the Vice-President will usually belong to the same party as the President. Many have doubted the wisdom of this change.

CHAPTER XLII.

THE 13TH, 14TH, AND 15TH AMENDMENTS.

1. In General.—These three amendments were the logical political result of the Civil War. Its ultimate cause was negro slavery; its final result, the raising of the negro to an equality before the law with the white man. These amendments differ from the others in this respect, that they are binding on the States as well as on the National Government. The States are named in them.

2. Slavery.—In 1863 President Lincoln had issued the Emancipation Proclamation. Whether this had any legal effect or not, the adoption of the 13th Amendment in 1865 did abolish slavery throughout the country **(98)**.

3. Civil Rights.—But it is evident that a person, though not a slave, may not have all the civil rights of others, as the right to acquire, hold, or sell property, to engage in trade, to live where he pleases, etc. The slaves, emerging from slavery, had no civil rights. But by the 14th Amendment they are made citizens and all civil rights bestowed upon them **(99)**. This was the second step in the elevation of the negro.

4. Apportionment of Representatives.—Thus 4,000,000 people were added to the number of citizens in the United States, and they should be represented in the House. Therefore the total population was made the basis of representation. But it was anticipated that the Southern States might not give the negro the right to vote, and thus he would be deprived of his representation in the House, while the white population of the South would derive all the gain from the increased representation, and therefore it was provided that whenever any State denied the suffrage to any male citizens of the United States, its Representatives should be proportionately decreased in number (**100**).

5. Political Disabilities.—We have seen that all officers of any State or the United States were required (**82**) to take an oath to support the Constitution. The North considered that engaging in war against the National Government was attempting to subvert the Constitution, and therefore a breach of that oath. Therefore it was thought best to deprive such as had taken the oath and afterward engaged in war against the Union of the right to hold office (**101**). But Congress was allowed to remove the disability, and has done so in case of all but a very few.

6. National Debt.—The 14th Amendment also recognizes and declares the validity of the national debt, but forbids the payment of any debt incurred in aid of rebellion, or any claim for the emancipation of the slaves (**102**). The South had incurred a large debt in the war, which was thus made void.

7. Right of Suffrage.—But though the colored race had all the civil rights, it had not as yet the right to vote. We have seen that the qualifications of voters is a matter belonging to the State (pages 26, 141, *note*). But by the 15th Amendment the State is forbidden to deny the right of suffrage to any one on account of his " race, color, or previous condition of servitude" (**103**). Thus the third and final step was taken in the constitutional changes, by which the black man was raised to a political equality with his fellow-man.

8. Final.—We have now completed our review of the National Government. The system established by the Constitution is peculiar, and is not necessarily suited to other countries. But as we study the Constitution our admiration for it should grow. The marvellous prosperity of the country, commercial and political, up to 1860, proved how well suited it was to our necessities, and the history of the four years between 1860 and 1865 has shown how severe a shock it may stand, for it is well grounded in the love of the people.

REVIEW QUESTIONS.

The National Government.

Origin and Nature.

1. How was this country governed prior to the Revolution?
2. State the causes of the Revolution.
3. State the political effect upon the Colonies of the Declaration of Independence.
4. When was the Confederation formed? How long did it last? State its principal defects.
5. State when the Union was formed. Its fundamental difference from the Confederation. The chief differences in detail.
6. What is the difference between a Confederacy and a Nation?
7. Give some instances showing the partial retention of the federative principle in the National Government.

Legislative Department.

8. Name the six objects of the Constitution stated in the preamble.
9. How many members are there in the House of Representatives? By whom elected? For what term? How apportioned among the States at first? How apportioned now? Qualifications?
10. Answer the same questions as to the Senate.
11. What is the object of two legislative houses?

12. Is the Senate or House of the higher dignity? Why?
13. How often does Congress meet? When? Define "A Congress."
14. By whom is impeachment made? By whom tried?
15. State the powers of each House as to its members, officers, quorum, adjournment, rules, journal, yeas and nays.
16. What privilege have members of Congress as to arrest? Why? As to liberty of speech? Why?
17. What bills may originate in the House? In the Senate?
18. State the reason for the provision as to revenue bills.
19. Name all the ways in which a bill, having passed both Houses, may become a law?
20. State the fundamental difference between Congress and a state legislature as to the origin and extent of their powers.
21. Name the subjects on which Congress may legislate.
22. What taxes may Congress lay? For what purposes?
23. From what source does most of the national revenue now come?
24. Why has Congress the power to regulate commerce? In what ways is it exercised? Explain retaliation duties.
25. What is Protection? Free Trade? State the chief argument for each. Which is the policy of the United States?
26. What is Registry of vessels? Clearance and Entry?
27. What is a citizen? An alien? Naturalization?
28. What is a bankrupt law? The power, why given to Congress?
29. State the powers of Congress as to coinage; as to weights and measures; as to the Post-Office. Why given?
30. What is a copyright? A patent? What are their objects?
31. What powers has Congress as to piracy? as to offences under international law? Why given?
32. Over what parts of the United States has Congress exclusive authority?
33. Name some of the implied powers of Congress.
34. Who has the power to declare war? Why?
35. What are letters of marque? What is prize?
36. How is an army raised? How does Congress control it?
37. By whom may the militia be called out? When?
38. Name the prohibitions upon the United States.
39. What is habeas corpus? A bill of attainder? An ex post facto law? An appropriation by Congress?
40. State the reason for the prohibitions as to titles of nobility.
41. Name the prohibitions upon the States.
42. State the difference between money and legal tender.
43. What is legal tender in the United States now?

Executive Department.

44. What is the advantage of having but one President?
45. By whom is he elected? For what term?
46. What other modes were proposed? State the objections to them? What was the purpose of the present one? Was its purpose accomplished? Why?

47. Are Presidential Electors elected or appointed? By whom? State their proceedings.
48. When does the House elect the President? How does it vote?
49. What are the President's qualifications? Salary?
50. What are the duties of the Vice-President?
51. State the President's powers as to the army and navy, reprieves and pardons, treaties, and appointments.
52. What is the danger connected with this power of appointment?
53. What is the purpose of the President's message?
54. What is the most comprehensive duty of the President?
55. Name the auxiliary executive departments, and their duties.

Judicial Department.

56. Explain the necessity for a national judiciary.
57. Name the national courts.
58. Can the United States be sued? Why?
59. What is the Court of Claims? How are its judgments enforced?
60. Are the judges appointed or elected? By whom? For what term?
61. State the three classes of cases in which the United States courts have jurisdiction, with the reason in each case.
62. What is treason? What proof necessary? Its punishment.
63. Name the crimes which the United States may punish.

Miscellaneous Provisions.

64. State the provision of the Constitution as to the rights of citizens of one State in another.
65. How are fugitive criminals returned?
66. What protection must the United States extend to the States?
67. How may the Constitution be amended?
68. When a law of Congress and a state law are antagonistic, which must prevail? A law of Congress and a state constitution?
69. What persons are obliged to take the oath to support the Constitution?
70. How did the Constitution originally become binding on a State? How does an amendment to it?
71. How many Amendments are there? What is the Bill of Rights? Its purpose?
72. State the substance of each amendment, when it was passed, and its purpose.
73. Can a State be sued by a State in a state court? In a national court?
74. Can a State be sued by a private person in a state court? In a national court? Why?

PART II.

PRINCIPLES OF LAW.

DIVISION I.

MUNICIPAL LAW.*

SECTION I.

CIVIL RIGHTS IN GENERAL.

CHAPTER XLIII.

ABSOLUTE CIVIL RIGHTS.†

1. Introductory.—In this Division, under the heading Municipal Law, it is our purpose to give a general idea of the ordinary civil rights secured to persons in the United States, and the principles of law by which they are protected. This is a subject which, being local, belongs in most part to the different States, and not to the National Government, but the principles are substantially the same in all the States.

---

* By this term is meant the body of laws governing the ordinary every-day actions of men, and their different rights in relation to each other; particularly as distinguished from international law. It might be used to mean law concerning cities, villages, etc., but that is not its meaning here (see page 16).

† See pages 15, 18.

2. Common Law.—There are two sources of law in this country, the *common law* and *statute law;* or the unwritten and written law. The Common Law of England is the basis of law in all the States except Louisiana. It is not a code of written laws enacted by a legislature, but consists of rules of action which have become binding from long usage and established custom. It is said to be founded in reason and the principles of justice. It was brought over from England by our ancestors, and established here before the Revolution; and is now the law in all particulars wherein the constitutions or legislatures have not changed it.

3. Statute Law.—But in each State the legislature is free to change the common law, and to legislate upon subjects which the common law does not touch. These laws enacted by the legislature are called *statutes;* from the Latin *statuo,* to fix or establish. For this reason the law on some subjects will differ in different States. Yet, as we have said before, the principles are the same.

4. Rights of Persons.—These have been before described as the three great rights of *personal security, personal liberty,* and *private property* (see page 15). We have seen what provisions are often contained in constitutions for their protection (Chap. XLI.). These are the fundamental rights of men, and most of the subordinate rights are but forms of one or another of these three.

5. Personal Security.—The right of personal security is also protected by the law which permits a person to exercise the natural right of self-defence. When assaulted so that one has reason to fear that he is in danger of his life or of some serious injury to body or limb, he may use all the force necessary in defence and may lawfully take the life of his assailant. It is lawful to take the life of a burglar found in a house at night, for he is presumed to be ready to commit murder. If the assault is not so violent as to cause one to fear serious injury, it is lawful to use only sufficient force to prevent the injury. But in all cases the offender may be sued for damages by the party injured. An assault is also punishable criminally. The right is further protected by the law, by which a man, on showing reasonable cause of danger of personal injury, may require his adversary to be bound with sureties to keep the peace.

6. Slander.—The right of personal security includes the right to be secure in our good names, and is protected by the law against slander and libel. A *slander* is a false statement about another which injures him in his reputation or business; such as, a charge that he has been guilty of a crime, or has a malignant disease, or any falsehood which he can prove has injured him. For uttering such falsehood the slanderer may be compelled to pay heavy damages to the injured person. And he is liable whether he originated the statement or merely repeated it. There is, however, no criminal punishment for slander.

7. Libel.—A libel is a false publication in print or writing, signs or pictures, tending to injure a person in his reputation or business, or to expose him to public hatred, contempt, or ridicule. And it is considered in law a publication of such defamatory writing, though communicated to a single person. A slander written or printed is likely to have a wider circulation, to make a deeper impression, and to become more injurious. Libel is therefore broader than slander, and a person may be liable in damages for words in print or writing for which he would not be liable if merely spoken. In case of libel, also, a person is not only liable to a private suit for damages, but may be indicted and tried as for other public offences, and it makes no difference whether he originates or merely repeats the statement.*

---

* It was formerly the law that in the criminal action for libel it made no difference whether the statement was true or false. The

8. Personal Liberty.—Every person has the right to go wherever he pleases, free from restraint on the part of others. If any one restrains him of his liberty even for a very short period or without violence, as by locking him in a room, he may recover damages. This is one of our most valued rights, and is forfeited only by crime. In children, lunatics, and others unable to care for themselves, it is limited in some degree, for their own good and that of the community. Before our late war the slaves had not this right, but now all are equal. The writ of Habeas Corpus has been referred to as one of the most efficient means of securing this right against false accusations of crime (page 85). Freedom of speech, of the press, and of religion are included in the term personal liberty. But it is a universal rule that one must not use his own rights so as to injure those of another. Thus one may not use his right of personal liberty in speaking of another so as to violate that other's right of personal security, i.e. by injuring his reputation.

9. Private Property.—Every person has the right to acquire, to use as his own, in any way he sees fit, and to dispose of, any amount of property. No one, not even the government, can deprive him of his property without his consent; though sometimes the government may take his property, when necessary for public use, by paying for it (page 70). This right of private property is fundamental, but it, too, is limited by the rule that one must use his own rights so as not to injure those of others. The purpose of law is to give to each one as much liberty as is consistent

---

reason was that the People were injured by the malicious statement, because, whether true or false, it excited the other party to commit some personal violence, and so commit a breach of the peace. But this is now changed in many States, and if the publication be true and published for a good purpose it is not a libel.

with the liberty of others. Sections II. and III. of this Division will contain a sketch of the system of law regulating and balancing the rights of property of all.

CHAPTER XLIV.

RELATIVE CIVIL RIGHTS.

a. Public.

1. Public Relative Civil Rights have been described before (page 15). Every person has the right to demand protection by the government. This protection is afforded by its police and other civil officers. So, also, if these are not sufficient the governor is bound to call out the militia, to protect even a single person. Another means of protection is the system of courts, in which every person is at liberty to sue in order to enforce his rights. In return for this protection the government is entitled to the obedience of the citizen. This is enforced in different ways. It may imprison, fine, or even kill one who disobeys its laws (Chap. LXI.).

b. Private.*

2. Duties of Parent.—Parents, as the natural protectors of their children, are obliged to provide for their support and education during their minority, or while they are under twenty-one years of age. The father, or, if there is no father, the mother, is bound to support the minor chil-

---

* The rights arising from the relation of husband and wife are treated of under Sec. II., Contracts, because marriage, the basis, is a contract (Chap. XLVI.).

dren. Even if they have property of their own, the father is so bound, but the mother is not. If a parent neglects to provide necessaries for his child, others may do so and sue the parent for their value.

3. Rights of Parent.—The parent has the right to the custody of his child, and, being deprived of it, may recover it again.* It is lawful for a parent to punish his child for good cause, but not cruelly. Being bound to provide for his children, the father has a right to their labor or service; and he may recover their wages from any person employing them without his consent. Children who are able are in general bound to support indigent parents.

4. Property of Child.—Very often a child has property of his own. As he is unable to take the management of it, a *guardian* is appointed for him for that purpose. The guardian may use the property for the support and education of the child (called his *ward*) during its minority. He may sell the personal property, but the real estate cannot be sold without permission from the court. At twenty-one the guardian must transfer all the property to his ward, and render an account of all his transactions. He is responsible for any loss caused by his wrong or negligence. If there is no parent, the guardian takes the place of parent to some extent, and has a right to the custody of his ward, and may administer proper punishment. If there is a father or mother, he or she is generally the one appointed guardian.

5. Apprenticeship.—This is a relation established by a written agreement, by which a male or female minor, with the consent of his or her parents, agrees to serve as an *apprentice*, or servant, to some one in a certain trade or employment, until twenty-one years of age, or for a less

---

* See page 85, note.

period. In return for these services the master is to teach the minor the trade. This is an exception to the rule of an infant's inability to contract (page 203), for the master can compel the apprentice to fulfill his agreement. To a certain extent he acts as a parent, may punish his apprentice, and is liable for his suport. The officers having charge of the poor may bind out pauper children in this way. Formerly apprenticeships were common, but now in this country they are little used, and the subject is an unimportant one in the law.

6. Master and Servant.—This relation can hardly be said to exist at present in this country. Formerly certain rights and duties flowed from it, such as the right of the master to administer corporal punishment, or the duty of the servant to protect his master against assailants. But, as a result of the democratic equality of all persons here, it has come to be merely a contract relation. The employer agrees to pay a certain sum for certain services which the employed agrees to render; and each must fulfill the contract (Chap. XLV.). With regard to how far an employer is answerable to other parties for the acts of the employed, the relation is one of principal and agent, and the principal is responsible just so far as the agent had a right to act for him (Chap. XLVII.).

SECTION II.

CONTRACTS.

CHAPTER XLV.

CONTRACTS IN GENERAL.

1. Definition.—A *contract* is an agreement or a promise by one person with another to do or not to do a particular thing. Contracts may be *written* or *oral*. Certain contracts, like those for the sale of land, must be in writing (see page 206); but most of the contracts of daily life are oral. They may be also *express* or *implied*. The former is where there is an agreement expressed orally or in writing; the latter is where a person does certain things which in law imply an agreement, as, where a person employs one to do anything for him, or buys certain things, a promise is implied to pay what the labor or the things bought are worth.* This subject of contracts is very broad in law, for most of our daily actions are but the fulfillment of contracts, and we may contract to do almost anything.

2. Rule.—The fundamental rule of law and justice with

---

* Another distinction between contracts is that they may be *executory* or *executed*. An executory contract is one where the agreement is to do something at some future time; an executed contract is one where nothing remains to be done afterward, but the agreement is immediately carried out. For instance: where one agrees to sell real estate at some future time the contract is executory; the deed itself is an executed contract.

regard to contracts is this: that a person must do what he or she has agreed to do. This is the rule, but the exceptions to it—also founded in justice—are quite numerous, and the principal ones will form the subjects of the following sections of this chapter.

3. Capacity of Parties.—It would be unjust to compel a person to fulfill his contracts if he were *incapable of contracting*; i.e. if his powers of thought were not strong enough to enable him to judge what was for his best advantage. For this reason infants (i.e. minors), lunatics, idiots, and some others, cannot be compelled to fulfill any contracts they may make. Otherwise great advantage might be taken of them by unscrupulous persons. But when one does contract with such a person, he cannot refuse to fulfill his share of the bargain, if the minor or other such person wishes to uphold it. Nor can the person incapable to contract, if he or she has received anything under the contract, refuse to fulfill it without restoring what has been received.

4. Infancy.—An *infant* in legal language is a person, boy or girl, under twenty-one years of age. The reason why they may not make contracts which may be enforced against them is that they have not had, as a rule, sufficient experience to prevent others from gaining the advantage in their contracts. Therefore an infant while he may receive property cannot sell any, and if he does, can regain it. But if after becoming of age he ratifies the contract, then it is as if he had made it when of age. There is one exception to an infant's incapacity to contract. He may contract for necessaries when he has no parent or guardian who supplies them; i.e. such things as food, clothing, lodging, and education, and when he obtains them may be made to pay for them. Otherwise he could not obtain them, for no one would trust him.

5. Lunacy.—Lunatics and idiots are protected in the same way, because they are unable to protect themselves. An agreement is an act of the mind, and therefore one who has no mind cannot, in reality, agree. A person while intoxicated has lost the use of his faculties for the time, and therefore any contract that he makes during that time he may refuse to fulfill; but, if he adopts it on becoming sober, he cannot afterward question it.

6. Married Women, by the common law, could not make contracts, and they cannot now in many particulars. This was not because of their supposed incapacity, but because the husband and wife were considered as one person. But the common law has been changed in many States by statute, and they may make some contracts; such as, any contract necessary in the management of their separate property, even to sell or buy it, and any contract made in connection with a business which they may be carrying on.

7. Assent.—Another requisite to a contract is the *mutual assent of the parties*. A mere offer by one party not assented to or accepted by the other constitutes no contract. This is implied in the word agreement, for it takes two to "agree." In case the parties are distant from each other, if the proposition is sent by mail, and a letter of acceptance is written and put in the mail, the contract is complete, unless, before mailing the letter of acceptance, a second letter has been received containing a retraction of the proposal.

8. Consideration.—Every contract must have a consideration to be enforceable.* The *consideration* of a contract is what is given, done, or promised, as the cause or

---

* Promissory notes and bills, transferred before they are due to a person who does not know whether they are without consideration or not, are an exception to this rule. (See page 224.)

reason for which a person enters into the agreement. Thus, the money given or promised, for which a man agrees to perform certain labor, is the consideration of the agreement. So the money or other thing for which a promissory note is given, is the consideration. Mutual promises are sufficient considerations to make a contract binding; but they must be made at the same time. Such promises support each other. The promise of one party constitutes a sufficient consideration for a promise by the other party. But the law will not enforce a contract on the part of one where the other party has not given, done, or promised something on his part. The purpose of the law is to remedy some injury done, but a party is not considered as injured when another refuses to fulfill a promise to him, unless he has done something on his part to balance such promise. Therefore promises wholly gratuitous are void, such as a promise to give one money or property as a gift.*

9. **Gratuitous Services.**—So, also, services rendered which have not been requested afford no ground for a claim for payment. This is a case not of lack of consideration, but of absence of contract. There is even no implied promise to pay for the services, for they were not requested. Had they been requested, there would have been an implied promise to pay for them. And it makes no difference how valuable the services are, as the saving of property from fire, or the securing of cattle found astray, or of property lost. This seems unjust, but the injustice would be greater were it the other way; for then any one might force any service upon us which we did not want, and compel us to pay for it.

---

* The moral law may require the fulfillment of such a promise, but the municipal law cannot. This is an instance where human law is not so broad as the moral law. (See page 17.)

10. Fraud and Force.—We have seen that assent is necessary to a contract. But it must also be given freely and with full knowledge. If it is obtained by means of force, as through threats of any kind, or by fraud, as by representing facts that were not true, or concealing facts that the other had a right to know, the party upon whom the force or fraud is practised can claim there is no contract if he wishes to. The other one cannot, for it is a rule in law that one cannot take advantage of his own wrong-doing.

11. Impossible Contracts.—No man can bind himself to do what is not in the power of man to do. But it is otherwise, if the thing to be done is only at the time impossible in fact, but not impossible in its nature, and this impossibility might have been anticipated. Hence, inability from sickness to fulfill an agreement, or the impossibility of procuring an article which a person has agreed to deliver, would not exempt him from liability in damages for the non-performance of his contract.

12. Illegal Contracts.—An agreement to do a thing that the law makes unlawful, such as to commit a crime, cannot be enforced, nor any promise made in consideration of such a contract. For this reason bets cannot be enforced in law, for betting and gaming are forbidden. But if a forbidden contract has been carried out, the law will not set it aside; it will not aid one wrong-doer as against another.

13. Written Contracts.—Any agreement is a contract and may be put in writing.* But there are certain agreements to which a person cannot be held against his will unless they are in writing and signed by him. The two

---

* When a contract is in writing neither party is allowed to prove that the real intention was different. The parties have put it in writing in order that it might be the best evidence of what the intention was.

principal classes are, a contract for the sale of real estate or any interest therein (deeds, leases,* etc.), and a contract for the sale of any personal property over a certain amount in value (pages 218, 237). Others are, an agreement to pay the debt of another, an agreement of an executor to pay the debt of an estate out of his own property, and any contract not to be performed within one year. Such transactions are important ones usually, and the evidence of them should be something less open to mistake than spoken words.

14. Limitations.—But though a contract might conform to all the requirements, it nevertheless could not be enforced unless an action were brought for the purpose within a particular time after it was made. This time varies, according to the nature of the action brought, from five or six years, as in the ordinary cases of debt, to twenty or thirty years, as in the case of land. Different States, too, have different periods for the same thing.

15. Remedies.—Where a contract is broken by one of the parties, the preventive remedies which the law gives to the other party are of two kinds: in cases where the wrong is not a single act but continuous, the court may order the wrong-doer to stop, as where one has agreed not to build a house on a particular spot but commences to do so; in certain kinds of cases the court may order one to fulfill his contract, or imprison him if he will not, as to sign a deed that he has agreed to give. But the compensatory remedy applies in nearly all cases, even in those where the others also apply. This remedy is to compel the party in the wrong to pay the party wronged so much money, called *damages*.

---

* Except in many States certain short leases (page 242).

CHAPTER XLVI.

MARRIAGE.

1. Its Nature.—Marriage is a contract. But it is also more than a contract or agreement: it is a permanent change of status, of condition. The rights of the parties toward each other are radically changed by marriage. This change was still greater in former generations than it now is. Being so important an act, the law does not allow it when either party is under a certain age, called the *age of consent*, because the person under that age is presumed to be too young to know what it really is that he or she is consenting to. Consent without knowledge of what is consented to is not real consent. In this chapter we are considering solely the contract *of* marriage, that is, marriage itself, which must not be confounded with the contract *to* marry at some future time, commonly called *engagement*.

2. Relationship.—Marriages between parties nearly related are forbidden, and if contracted are, in general, void. The laws of the States differ as to the degree of relationship at which persons may not marry. The most common rule is that first cousins may, but any more nearly related may not. Thus a marriage between uncle and niece is void.

3. Lunacy: Force: Fraud.—As in all other contracts, to make a marriage binding the parties must act freely, and must have sufficient intelligence to know what they are doing. If one is forced to marry by threats or other means, the marriage may be declared void if the party forced so desires. So the lunatic or idiot, or some one representing him or her, may have the marriage declared void. In those cases the other party cannot complain, and the marriage is binding if the forced or incapable person desires it to be.* But if one is deceived into marrying a lunatic, that is fraud, and it entitles him to have the marriage annulled. So, also, if a party marries one, thinking it is another. In all these cases there is no real consent, and hence no contract.

4. Ceremony.—There is usually no definite form which must be followed in the performance of marriage, and no particular words which the parties must use. The only essential part is that they acknowledge, in seriousness and in some appropriate manner, that they marry each other. It is always prudent, if not necessary, that this should be done in the presence of a number of witnesses, for otherwise there might be no one to prove the marriage. The laws of many States provide that the ceremony must be performed by a clergyman, or some judicial or other officer. Any one who saw a marriage performed may prove it in court.

5. Bigamy.—This is marriage with a second, while still possessing a first husband or wife. Not only is it a crime for which one may be punished, but such second marriage is null and void. It has no effect on the first marriage. Polygamy is marriage with more than two. In such case all marriages but the first are void. The polygamy practised by the Mormons in Utah is contrary to the laws of the United States.

6. The Wife's Property.—By the common law the property which a woman owned became her husband's on marriage. Her personal property became his absolutely, and he might use and dispose of it as he pleased. Her real estate he could not dispose of, but had the right to use it

---

* See page 206, sec. 10.

while they both lived. It will be seen how dependent on her husband she became. This was the rule once, but one part of it after another has been changed, until at present in most States the wife retains the use and right of disposal of all her property, both real and personal, as though she were single.

7. Dower.—Such were the rights he gained in her property. But by the common law she obtained a certain right in his property, but only his real estate. This right, called *dower*, is the right of the wife upon the death of her husband to have set apart, for her own use during her life, one-third part of all the real estate which the husband possessed at any time during marriage. During his life she could not claim it, but might on his death, though he had sold the land. This right still exists in most of the States. This is the reason why a wife must join with her husband in signing a deed (see page 237). Its object is to prevent a husband leaving his wife destitute.

8. Support.—The husband is bound to maintain his wife, and is liable for debts which she may contract for necessaries, but for nothing more. If he refuses to provide for her wants, or if, through other ill-treatment or fault on his part, they become separate, he is liable to fulfill her contracts for necessaries, even though he has forbidden persons to trust her. If she leaves him by her own fault, or if they part by consent, and he secures to her a separate maintenance, and pays it according to agreement, he is not liable even for necessaries.

9. Divorce.—No length of separation while both parties live, nor any consent, can dissolve the marriage contract. The only way to dissolve it is by a decree of a court granting a *divorce*. The most common cause for which this may be obtained is adultery, but some States allow it for other causes, such as desertion, cruelty, drunkenness.

After the divorce the innocent party is at liberty to marry again. The guilty party may not by the laws of some States.*

CHAPTER XLVII.

PRINCIPAL AND AGENT.

1. Nature of Agency.—An *agent* is a person authorized to act with third parties on behalf of and in the name of another, who is called the *principal.* This is one of the most common and necessary relations of life, and exists with regard to all kinds of subjects. Every clerk, employé, or laborer is the agent of the person or corporation that employs him, so far as what he does is in connection with third parties. All brokers and officers of corporations act almost wholly as agents in their business. So, also, do lawyers, auctioneers, masters of ships, etc.

2. Act of Agent.—The fundamental rule of agency is that a principal is bound by the acts of his agent, as if they were his own acts, so long as the agent keeps within the authority granted him. If that authority is exceeded the principal is not bound, unless he afterward ratify the act. †

---

* *Limited divorces* are also granted sometimes, but these do not permit either party to marry again.

A divorce proper must be distinguished from that judgment of a court which annuls a marriage on the ground of force, fraud, incapacity, or want of age. The latter kind of decree, though often called a divorce, decides that there never was any legal marriage, for some cause existing prior to the supposed marriage; a divorce proper dissolves a binding legal marriage for some cause arising after it.

† If in any case an agent appears to have a general authority, which is really limited by private instructions, the principal is re-

3. Wrong Committed by Agent.—This power of an agent to bind his principal extends not only to the making of contracts or other business acts, but even to the committing of personal injuries, if they are committed in connection with the business: thus, if the engineer of a railroad train through negligence injures any person or property, the company is responsible. But the wrong must have been committed in connection with the business in which the agent is employed. If there is no connection between the act and the employment, it is only the personal act of the agent, and he alone is liable.

4. Duty to Principal.—The relation between the agent and principal alone is one of contract, the agreement being on the agent's part that he will act as the principal directs, with care, skill, and diligence. Therefore an agent is bound, in general, to observe the instructions of his principal, even though an act contrary to such instructions should be intended, and really be, for the benefit of the principal. The agent must bear, personally, all losses growing out of a non-compliance with his orders; and the profit accruing therefrom goes to the benefit of the principal. When an agent receives no instructions, he must conform to the usage of trade or to the custom applicable to the particular agency.

5. Liability to Third Parties.—When an agent is duly authorized to do an act—not unlawful in itself, such as a crime or misdemeanor—he is not responsible to third parties (i.e. those with whom he deals) for that act. The principal alone is bound, for he is the one who derives the benefit. But there are three principal cases in which an agent acting for another makes himself liable: (1) where

---

sponsible for any act which comes within the apparent authority, though it may not be within the real authority.

he exceeds his authority;* (2) where he professes to act as agent, but does not disclose his principal; and (3) where he is really acting as agent, but professes to be acting for himself. The rule is general that if an agent fails to bind his principal he binds himself. In the second and third cases, where the principal is not known, the agent is bound, because otherwise the party with whom he deals might have no one that he could hold responsible to him: but in such cases he may hold the principal also, if he is discovered, for one cannot take the benefit of an act without being bound by it.

6. Commission Merchants.—This class of agents is quite large in cities. A commission merchant is one who sells for another the goods manufactured or raised by the latter, for a compensation, usually a percentage on the price (called a *commission*). Very often they sell without disclosing the name of their principals. All the appropriate rules of agency apply to them, as to personal liability or non-liabililityy, care, skill, etc.

7. Lien.—Though the goods which a commission merchant sells belong to some one else, he has a *lien* upon them for any advances he has made to the owner,† and for his expenses and commissions. A lien on personal property is a right to hold it against the owner; that is, the owner cannot take the goods away without refunding the money received and paying any charge due. Even though the owner should order him not to sell, the commission merchant may sell in order to satisfy his claim, paying over the surplus, if any, to the owner. There are also other kinds of liens on property (see pages 218, 229, 232).

---

* But if the third party knows that the agent has no authority, the agent is not bound. No one is.

† It is very common for the commission merchant to advance a portion of the price to the owner, before sale.

8. Brokers.—These form another common class of agents. A *broker* is an agent employed chiefly to negotiate sales between parties. His business may consist in negotiating exchanges; or in buying and selling stocks, goods, ships, or cargoes; or in procuring insurances and settling losses, etc.; and as he confines himself to one or the other of these branches, he is called an exchange broker, stock broker, insurance broker, etc. A broker differs from a commission merchant in that the former has not the custody of the goods of his principal. He is merely empowered to effect the contract of sale; and when this is done his agency ends. As to his principal he must carry out his agreement; i.e. must do what he agrees with skill, care, and promptness. As to others he is subject to all the rules of agency.

CHAPTER XLVIII.

PARTNERSHIP.

1. Definition.—A partnership is an association formed by contract between two or more persons for joining their money, labor, or skill, in lawful business, the profits to be divided and the loss to be borne by the partners in certain proportions. It is a partnership if one furnishes the funds and the other performs the labor; or if, when no money is necessary, each agrees to do his share of the labor. A partnership is often denominated a *firm*, or *house*. It is very often formed by written *articles of partnership*, but it may be formed by an oral agreement.

2. Act of One Partner.—The great rule of partnership is that the act of one partner binds all. In matters pertaining to the business of the firm, each partner is the agent of the firm; so that if one buys or sells for the firm, all are bound. Not only the property owned by the firm and used in the business, but also the private property of each partner, is liable for the debts of the firm. But this authority of each partner to act for the partnership extends only to the business in which they are engaged; if one acts in the name of the firm. in any other matter, he is an agent without authority, and therefore binds only himself (page 212, sec. 5).

3. **Secret Partner.**—One who should conceal his name so as not to be known as a partner when the debt is contracted, may be sued when discovered to be such. This is the case of an undisclosed principal (page 213).

4. **Transfer of Interest.**—A partner cannot sell his interest to another person, who is to take his place in the partnership, without the consent of all the partners. The power of a partner is so great that each one ought to have the right in the beginning to say who shall exercise this right for him. Whenever a new member is taken in, or an old member retires, it is really the formation of a new firm.

5. **Duration.**—The contract of partnership may be for any specified time, or no particular time may be specified. In the former case it cannot be dissolved before the time expires, except by a court for some misconduct on the part of one partner, or for his insanity or other inability. In the latter case, where no time is fixed, any partner may at will dissolve the partnership. The death of one partner dissolves it.

6. **Notice of Dissolution.**—When a partnership is dissolved by the withdrawal of any of the partners, notice of dissolution must be given, for a firm may be bound by a contract made by one partner, in the usual course of business and in the name of the firm, with the person who contracted on the faith of the partnership, and who had no

notice of the dissolution.* The same notice is necessary to protect a retiring partner from continued responsibility. And even if due notice is given, yet, if he willingly suffers his name to continue in the firm or in the title of the firm over the door of the shop or store, he may in certain cases be liable.

7. **Limited Partnership.**—In some of the States, a partnership may be formed by a number of persons, some of whom are to be responsible only to a limited amount; and their names are not to be used in the firm. Before a partnership of this kind can do business, a writing and certificate signed by the parties stating the terms of partnership and the amount for which the *special partners* (as they are called) are to be responsible must be recorded. The terms of partnership must also be published in a newspaper. In these *limited* partnerships, as they are termed, the special partners are liable only to the amount stated in the terms of partnership. The other partners, called *general partners*, whose names only are used, and who transact the business, are liable for all the debts contracted, as in ordinary partnerships.

8. **Rights as to Each Other.**—So far we have treated only of the rights of partners as to third parties. As to each other they have just such rights as they may agree upon. It is wholly a matter of contract. Thus a partner may sell an article to a third person when he has not the right to do it as to his partners, because he has agreed with them not to do so. In partnerships containing more than two, a majority usually has the right to decide all questions.

---

* Actual notice must be given to those dealing regularly with the firm, but as to the rest of the world a publication in some newspaper is sufficient.

CHAPTER XLIX.

SALES OF PERSONAL PROPERTY.

1. Definition of Sale.—A sale is a contract by which the ownership (called the *title*) of certain property is transferred from one person to another for a certain price: the exchange of a commodity for its equivalent in money. The exchange of one commodity for another is *barter*. The same general principles of law which apply to contracts in general are applicable to contracts of sale; viz., the competency of the parties to contract; the assent of the parties; the absence of fraud; the sufficiency of the consideration; its possibility and legality.

2. Existence of Property.—A thing cannot be sold unless it exists. Thus, if A sells a horse or certain goods to B, and if, at the time of the sale, the horse is dead or the goods are destroyed, the sale is void.*

3. Agreement to Sell.—But a person may agree to sell at some future time an article not now in existence or which he does not own, for he may manufacture or buy it. Such an agreement is subject to all the ordinary rules of contracts. It is an executory contract; while a sale is an executed contract.

4. Delivery.—To constitute a valid sale, as between the seller and buyer, it is not necessary that the articles should be delivered. By the contract alone—if it is valid in other respects, such as being without fraud, or in writing if necessary—they become the buyer's property, and it is his

---

* But one may sell that which is the expected product or increase of something to which the seller has a present right. Thus, a man may sell the wool that may grow on his sheep, the fruit that may grow on his trees, or the future increase of his cattle.

loss if they are destroyed before delivery. Sale and delivery are thus two separate acts. In case of barter, however, the delivery must be made before the ownership will change.

5. Written Contract.—In certain cases some memorandum in writing of the terms of the sale must be signed by the party to be charged, or his authorized agent, or he can repudiate the sale. These cases are any sales of personal property over a certain amount in value, varying in the different States from $30 to $200. No writing is necessary when the goods are under the fixed amount in value; and even when over that amount it is not necessary if there is (1) a delivery and acceptance by the buyer of some part of the goods sold, or (2) a payment of any part of the price.

6. Lien.—When nothing is said at the sale as to the time of delivery or the time of payment, the buyer is entitled to the goods on payment or tender of the price, and not otherwise; for though he acquires the *right of property* by the contract of sale, he does not acquire the *right of possession* until he pays or tenders the price. This right of the seller to hold the goods until paid is called his *lien*. But if the seller delivers the goods absolutely, and without fraudulent contrivance on the part of the buyer, he loses his lien. All he then has is the right to sue the buyer for the price. But when goods are sold on credit and nothing is said as to the time of delivery, the buyer is immediately entitled to the possession.

7. Sale without Title.—Where one professes to sell what he does not own, no ownership passes, even though he has it in possession and the buyer has no suspicion that it is not his. The true owner can claim the property at any time. This is so whether the article was lost or stolen from him.

8. Exception.—Money and what is called negotiable

paper * form an exception to this rule. If they are sold or transferred, even by a thief, to one who gives good consideration for them, and has no reason to suspect they do not belong to the one professing to own them, they belong to the buyer, and the true owner loses them.

9. Warranty of Title.—In the sale of personal property, if the seller has possession of the article and sells it as his own, he is understood to *warrant the title;* that is, he in effect agrees to reimburse the buyer if some third person proves the article to be his. This agreement is implied whether anything is said about it or not. But if the possession is at the time in another, and there is no express covenant or warranty of title, the party buys at his peril, and cannot look to the seller for reimbursement. If, however, the seller affirms that the property is his own, he warrants the title, though it is not in his possession.

10. Quality.—With regard to the *quality* of the thing, the seller is not bound to make good any deficiency, unless he expressly warranted the goods to be of a certain quality, or unless he made a fraudulent representation or concealment concerning them. The rule is, if there is no express warranty by the seller, nor fraud on his part, and if the article is equally open to the inspection of both parties, the buyer who examines the article for himself must abide by all losses arising from its not being what he wanted or expected.

---

* "Negotiable paper" includes bank-bills, bonds of the National or State Governments, of cities, railroads, etc., when payable to bearer, stock certificates with blank powers of attorney attached, promissory notes and bills endorsed in blank or payable to bearer, and some other securities.

CHAPTER L.

GIFTS: FRAUDULENT TRANSFERS.

1. Gifts.—In general a person may, if he wishes, give away any or all of his property to any one, without receiving anything in return. But delivery is necessary to a gift. When delivered, the gift cannot be revoked by the giver, but a mere promise to give cannot, we have seen, be enforced (page 205). There is one exception to this rule: a gift made in anticipation of the death of the giver may be revoked by him at any time before death.

2. Creditors' Rights.—But if a man is insolvent, or is in such embarrassed circumstances that he is likely soon to become insolvent, he is not allowed to give away any of his property. His creditors have a right to have it applied to the payment of their debts. If the creditors do not complain, the gift remains irrevocable.

3. Delivery of Personal Property.—We have seen that delivery is not necessary to a valid sale as between the buyer and seller (page 217). But when it is not delivered, this gives the seller an opportunity to defraud by selling it over again, or to deceive his creditors by pretending he has sold or mortgaged it when he really has not. For this reason, the law in some States provides that a sale or mortgage of personal property without delivery shall be void as against creditors and subsequent purchasers; that is, the creditor or second purchaser can take it in spite of the first sale.

4. Chattel Mortgages.*—Persons very often wish to borrow money, and mortgage some personal property for its payment and yet retain and use the property. This, however, would be impossible if the rule given in section 3

---

* Chattel means personal property.

were absolute. Provision is therefore made in many States by which these mortgages may be recorded in the town or county clerk's office, and when so recorded the mortgage is valid against any one, though the property is left with the owner.

5. Transfers to Creditors.—A debtor may transfer his property to a creditor in payment of his debt, even though it leaves other debts unpaid. It is also a very common occurrence for a person in failing circumstances to assign all his property, in trust, to one or more persons, who are to dispose of it, and to apply the avails to the payment of his creditors, or a part of them. He may in such assignment direct that certain ones shall be paid first. But such an assignment does not release the debtor from his debts, unles the property is sufficient to pay them in full.

6. Releases.—It is also common for creditors to release their debtor on payment of a part of the debt. Such release is valid if signed and sealed. When a debtor agrees to pay his creditors a certain proportion of their claims in consideration of a discharge of their demands, if he privately agrees to give a better or further security to one than to others, the contract is void as to all; because the condition upon which they agree to discharge the debtor is that they shall share equally.

CHAPTER LI.

PROMISSORY NOTES AND BILLS OF EXCHANGE.

a. Notes.

1. A Promissory Note is a written promise to pay a specified sum of money at a certain time, to a person named, or to his order, or to the bearer. The following is a common form:

$100.   NEW YORK, May 28, 1880.

Three months after date, I promise to pay to James Smith & Co., or order, one hundred dollars, value received.

JOHN BROWN.

In such a note, Brown is the *maker*, and Smith & Co. the *payees*. The words "value received" have generally little legal force.

b. Bills.

2. A Bill of Exchange* (called also a *draft*) is a written order or request by one person to another to pay a third person a certain sum of money. The following is a common form:

$1000.   NEW YORK, May 28, 1880.

Twenty days after date (or at sight, or ten days after sight), pay to the order of James Smith & Co. one thousand dollars, value received;
and charge the same to account of   THOMAS JONES.
  To JOHN BROWN,
    New Orleans, La.

In such a bill, Jones is the *drawer*, Smith & Co. the *payees*, and Brown the *drawee*. After acceptance, the drawee is called the *acceptor*.

3. Use of Bills.—Bills are of very great convenience in commerce. Suppose Jones, of New York, owes Smith & Co., of New Orleans, $1000; and that Brown, of New Orleans owes Jones $1000. If Jones sends Smith & Co. an

---

* In this chapter we shall call it a *bill*.

order upon Brown to pay $1000 to them, both debts are cancelled, and the trouble and danger of sending the money is avoided. Smith & Co. may transfer the bill to any one before payment, in which case they become indorsers (see sec. 7).

4. Acceptance.—The bill is presented to the drawee before it becomes due. If, when presented, he agrees to pay it when due, he is said to *accept* the bill, and writes his acceptance upon it. An acceptance may, however, be oral. A drawee is under no obligation to the payee to accept, but, having accepted, he becomes the principal debtor; and the drawer becomes a surety; that is, he agrees to pay if the acceptor does not. The acceptor is bound, though he accepted without consideration and for the sole accommodation of the drawer.

5. Non-Acceptance.—If the drawee refuses to accept, the indorsers become liable to the holder and to each other in their order for the amount of the bill, as described in section 14, provided notice of the non-acceptance is sent them, as described in section 16. So, also, if the bill is not paid when due they become liable in the same way, if notice is sent.

6. Check.—A check upon a bank is a bill of exchange, and is subject to all the appropriate rules. It is usually payable on demand, and has no days of grace.

c. *Rules applicable to both.*

7. Indorsement.—A note or bill payable to bearer may be transferred by delivery without any writing; but when payable to the order of any one, it is usually transferred by the one to whose order it is made writing his name at the time of delivery across the back. This is called *indorsement*. The indorsement is considered as the order of the payee to the maker or acceptor to pay it to some other person. A bill may be indorsed before or after acceptance. Where the name simply is written across the back it is called a *blank indorsement*, and it may thereafter be transferred from one to another by delivery, the same as one payable to bearer. Or the payee may order it paid to any particular person. Such person may in turn make it payable to bearer by indorsing in blank, or may make it payable to any particular person. He thus becomes the second indorser, the payee being the first. In case of a bill the drawer is a surety to both. The person in whose hands it is when due collects it.*

8. Notes and Bills are Contracts, and therefore as between the original parties (in a note the maker and payee, in a bill the acceptor and payee) they must conform to all the rules governing contracts, as to consideration, legality, etc. (Chap. XLV.). Thus if—in above note—Brown had received nothing for it from Smith & Co., but he had given it to them in order that they might sell it to some one else and thus raise money, they could not sue him upon it.† So, also, if he had any claim against them, he could offset it against the note. But as soon as Smith & Co. indorse the note or bill and sell it to some one else, it is no longer subject to those rules, as will be explained in the following section.

9. Negotiability.—When a note or bill has been thus transferred, before it is due, to some one who gives money or other consideration for it, and who has no knowledge of how it originated, such an owner may collect it from the maker or acceptor, although the payee could not. Thus

---

* The advantage of making notes, checks, and bills payable to order is that no one but the one to whose order they are payable can collect, and if lost the owner suffers no loss. It is otherwise with those payable to bearer or indorsed in blank (see sec. 9).

† Such notes are quite common, called *accommodation notes*.

the maker or acceptor cannot plead that he received no consideration for it, nor that it has been paid, though those matters should be true. He cannot offset against it any demand he has against one who did own it. In case of a note or bill payable to bearer or indorsed in blank, even though it had been stolen from an owner, a person receiving it in good faith could collect it, and the real owner could not. This is an exception to the rule that the true owner of stolen property is entitled to it wherever he finds it (see page 218). Hence, notes and bills are called *negotiable paper*. But if the holder has knowledge of any of these defects, or if he has reason to suspect their existence, he cannot sue the maker or acceptor on it.

10. Reason for It.—The reason for this difference between negotiable paper and other contracts is its common use, and the facility with which it passes from one to another. Its use in commercial transactions is of great public convenience, one note sometimes passing through five or six hands; and it is proper that, for the sake of trade, protection should be given to the holder of such paper who receives it fairly in the way of business. But it could not be so used if each holder had to take the risk of there being some defence to it of which he could know nothing. But it is also proper to refuse aid to one who takes it with knowledge of its defects.

11. Transfer after Maturity.—After falling due a note or bill is no longer negotiable. If transferred after maturity, the maker or acceptor may make any defence to it he could have made as against the person who owned it at maturity. For instance: in case of a note, if the payee owned it when due and there was no consideration for it originally, the maker need not pay it. But if the one who owns it when due can collect it, any one to whom he transfers it can also. The general rule is that one can always convey the rights he has. A transfer of negotiable paper before maturity is peculiar, in that it may convey rights that the person transferring did not have.

12. Time of Payment: Interest.—Notes and bills payable *on demand*, or in which no time of payment is mentioned, are due immediately, and no demand of payment is necessary. But a note payable *at sight*, or at a specified time after sight, must be presented for payment before it can be sued. If the words "with interest" are omitted, interest commences at the time the note or bill becomes due. If payable on demand, it will draw interest from the time when payment is demanded.

13. Days of Grace.—Notes and bills payable by their terms on a certain day are not really due until the third day thereafter. Those three days are called *days of grace*. If the last day of grace falls on Sunday or a legal holiday, it is due the day before.

14. Indorser's Liability. — Indorsement is a contract. Whenever a person to whom a note or bill is made payable, or one to whom it has been indorsed, writes his name on the back and transfers it to another, he contracts with that other and with all future holders that if the maker or acceptor does not pay it when due, he will. Therefore the holder of an unpaid note may sue not only the maker or acceptor, but every indorser whose name is on the back when he takes it. In case of an accepted bill the holder may sue the acceptor, the indorsers, and drawer. In case of a non-accepted bill he may sue the indorsers and drawer. If an indorser pays it, he may sue any indorser prior to him, besides the maker, and in case of a bill the acceptor and drawer. One who transfers a note or bill, payable to bearer or indorsed in blank, is not liable to any one on it.

15. Demand of Payment.—The maker of a note or acceptor of a bill may be sued at any time after maturity, whether payment was demanded or not. But to hold the indorsers of a note, or the indorsers and drawer of an accepted bill, responsible, payment must be demanded of the maker or acceptor on the last day of grace.

16. Notice to Indorser.—If the maker or acceptor does not pay on that day, notice of that fact must be given to the indorsers and drawer to hold them; and the whole of the next day is allowed in which to send the notice. But the holder need only notify such as he chooses to hold liable to him, in which case if the indorser notified wishes to hold prior ones liable to him, he must himself send them notices, which he has another day to do. If the holder notifies all (the usual course), they are liable in their order to each other.* It is not necessary that the notice should reach the party for whom it is intended, but simply that it should be left at his residence if the parties live in the same town, or sent by mail if they do not.

17. Forged Paper.—If a note or bill is forged, no one can gain any right upon it against the one whose name is forged. So if an indorsement is forged it conveys no right, or if the amount is raised by forgery. This is so, although a person should buy it in good faith believing it genuine. Negotiability only applies to true instruments. On the same principle, in those States where a usurious contract is wholly void, a usurious note or bill is void in the hands of every one.

---

* The object of the notice is to give the indorser the earliest opportunity to secure himself against loss.

CHAPTER LII.

SERVICES.

1. Kinds of Service.—A very common class of contracts is that where one party undertakes to perform some labor or service for another. The services of doctors, lawyers, editors, the different kinds of manufacturers and mechanics, such as carpenters, painters, tailors, etc., belong to this class. Very often there is no express agreement to pay, but a request for the labor is sufficient, and a contract to pay a reasonable price for it is implied.

2. Ordinary Skill.—By undertaking to render such services a person represents that he has the ordinary skill and knowledge necessary in the trade or profession, and if he has not he can recover nothing for his labor, and is liable for all damage done. Thus a doctor who injures one through neglect or want of skill or knowledge is answerable for all damage.

3. Care of Property.—When the property of one person comes into the hands of another, for safe-keeping, repair, or other purpose, he must take such care of it as an ordinarily careful man does of his own property. The degree of care must be in proportion to the advantage he is to derive from it. Thus a borrower, who pays nothing for its use, must exercise the greatest care; ordinary care is required of one who expends labor on it and receives an equivalent, or of a hirer, or of one who takes it as a pledge for debt; slight care is sufficient when the party having it derives no advantage. In all these cases, if the property is lost or injured, but through no fault of the person having it, it is the owner's loss.

4. Hotel-Keepers are obliged to take all who apply to

them for lodging or board and offer to pay their regular price. They are in general responsible for all injuries to the goods and baggage of their guests, even for thefts. But for loss caused by unavoidable accident, or by superior force, as robbery, they are not liable. They have a lien upon the baggage of their guests for the payment of their charges.

5. Common Carriers are those who transport goods for hire as a common business, whether by land or by water. All railroad, steamboat, express, and stage companies are common carriers. They are bound to receive, from any person paying or tendering the freight charges, such goods as they are accustomed to carry and as are offered for the place to which they carry. But they may refuse to receive them if full, or if they are dangerous to be carried.

6. The Responsibility of common carriers is greater than that of others who receive property not their own for some purpose, such as mechanics, manufacturers, depositaries, etc. The latter we have seen are not responsible for the loss or injury of the property, except when it occurs through some degree of neglect on their part; but the common carrier is responsible in all cases, whether negligent or not. He is, in effect, an insurer of the goods against any loss or injury. But if it occurs through some great event which could not have been anticipated, like an inundation, war, etc., he is not liable.

7. As to Passengers the responsibility of common carriers is not so great. They are only liable for injuries which occur through the want of skill, knowledge, or care, of themselves or their agents.

8. Lien.—Where the personal property of one comes into the hands of another, for the performance of some labor in connection with it, the latter has a *lien* upon it for his services; that is, he may retain it until paid. Thus a carriage-maker has a lien upon the carriage he has repaired; a blacksmith upon the horse he has shod; and a common carrier upon the goods he has transported. They have also the right to enforce the contract by suit. But if they allow the property to go out of their possession they lose the lien.

CHAPTER LIII.

INSURANCE.

1. Kinds.—Contracts of insurance are of three kinds, fire, marine, and life insurance, and are usually in writing. They are called *policies*, and are generally issued by an incorporated company, in return for a fixed yearly payment, called a *premium*. Being merely contracts, they are subject to all the ordinary rules governing contracts. As a rule, the premium must be paid on the day when due, or the insurance ceases. We will refer only to a few points in which they are peculiar.

2. Fire.—A contract of fire insurance is an agreement to pay for the loss or injury by fire of certain property, real or personal, during a certain period. This includes all damage done to the property not only by the fire itself, but also in consequence of a fire. Thus if it be injured by water used to put out the fire, even though it is not in the same building, the insurers are liable. The policy usually names a certain amount, and the company is liable for all damage up to that amount. But the owner must do all he can to save the property.

3. Marine.—A contract of marine insurance is an agreement to pay for the loss or injury of a vessel, or the goods carried in it, through shipwreck, fire, piracy, or other peril of the sea. Sometimes the property insured is named as of a certain value, in which case neither party, in case of loss, can prove it to be otherwise. Marine is different from fire insurance in this particular, that if the vessel or cargo is damaged to at least one-half its value, the owner may give up what remains to the company and claim a total loss. This is called *abandonment*. In fire insurance this cannot be done except by special agreement.

4. Life.—A contract of life insurance is an agreement to pay a certain person a certain sum of money at the death of another, or when the latter reaches a certain age. Very often a husband is said to insure his life by a policy payable to his wife, but in reality in such case the contract is between the company and the wife. So one may insure his life in his own favor, in which case the policy is payable to his legal representatives.

5. Interest.—The person with whom the company contracts must have some ownership or interest in the subject of insurance. Thus in fire and marine insurance if any one but an owner, mortgagee, or other person having claim upon the property makes such a contract, it is void, being merely a wager, and all wagering contracts being illegal. So, in life insurance, the person to whom the money is to be paid must be dependent in some way for support upon the one at whose death it is to be paid, or must be a creditor, in order to have an insurable interest.

6. Several Policies are often issued by different companies covering the same property. In fire insurance they usually bear only a ratable proportion of the loss. In marine insurance it is often provided in the policy that the company shall only be liable for such portion of the loss as prior insurance does not satisfy.

7. Representations, made at the time the insurance is

taken, if known to be false, make the contract void. This is a general rule of contracts, but is unusually important in insurance. In marine insurance there is always a warranty, implied if not expressed, that the vessel insured, or on which the insured goods are shipped, is seaworthy; that is, able to withstand the ordinary dangers of the sea.

CHAPTER LIV.

SHIPPING.

1. In General.—The rules of law applicable to shipping are in many respects the same as those governing other subjects; namely, the ordinary rules of contracts, sales, agency, etc. But the property and the situation in which it is placed are often peculiar, from which peculiar rules arise. A few of these we will speak of.

2. Loss of Goods.—The responsibility of carriers by sea for loss or injury of the goods is not so great as that of inland common carriers. They are not liable when it is caused by some extraordinary peril of the sea, as a violent storm, fire, piracy, etc.; but if caused by the unseaworthiness of the vessel, want of equipment, or through some fault of those navigating it, they are liable.

3. Lien.—This is a common right in connection with a vessel. The carrier has a lien on the goods he transports for his freight: the owner of the goods has a lien upon the vessel for any claim he has for breach of the contract, loss of the goods, etc.; the seamen have a lien on the vessel for their wages; and any person who furnishes work or materials in the repairing or equipment of a foreign vessel has a lien upon it for what is due. This lien is a right to have the vessel sold, if necessary, to satisfy the claim. It is not like the common law lien, which is a right to retain property (page 229).

4. A Bill of Lading is a document delivered by the master (or owners) of a vessel to one shipping goods upon it, acknowledging their receipt for transportation. The person shipping the goods sends this to the one to whom they are sent. The latter may transfer it to another, indorsing it either in blank or to some particular person, as in notes and bills (page 223). This transfers the ownership of the goods; and the final holder of the bill of lading may demand the goods when they arrive.

5. General Average.—Whenever any portion of a vessel or its cargo is voluntarily destroyed or thrown overboard at sea by the master, in a case of necessity, in order to save the rest, and the rest is saved thereby, all the owners of the vessel and the cargo must bear a portion of the loss in proportion to the value of their property there. This is called *general average*. Its reason is evident, that all obtain the benefit. It is very common for part of a cargo to be thrown overboard to lighten a ship, but it would be unjust to make the owner of that portion bear all the loss, when otherwise both vessel and cargo would have been lost.

6. Salvage.—If one vessel finds another vessel or goods upon the sea, deserted or in great danger, and saves them, a large proportion of the property, or its value, is distributed among the owner, master, and crew of the saving vessel. This proportion is often one-third to one-half. It is called *salvage*, and its object is to encourage the rendering of such services.

7. Master's Authority.—The master of a vessel has complete authority over the crew and passengers when at sea. He may use force to compel obedience in the management of the vessel, and may even take life when necessary. When necessary for the safety of the vessel or cargo, he may sell or mortgage both.

CHAPTER LV.

INTEREST.

1. Definition.—Interest is a premium paid for the use of money lent. To be interest it must be a return for money lent, and not a profit on money invested. Thus dividends upon railroad or other stock, or the profits of a business, are not interest.

2. Rate.—Each State declares by law what shall be its legal rate of interest. This varies in the different States from six to ten per cent per annum, being six in most.

3. Usury.—The taking by the creditor of a rate of interest beyond that which is established by law is *usury*. Parties may freely contract to take less than the legal rate; but when more is contracted for, not only can no more be collected on the contract or obligation than the legal rate, but in most of the States there is some additional forfeiture. In a few the obligation is void, and the payment of no part of the debt can be enforced by law; in others, twice or thrice the excess above the lawful interest is forfeited; and in some only the excess paid can be recovered.

SECTION III.

REAL ESTATE.

CHAPTER LVI.

ESTATES IN REAL PROPERTY.

1. Estate, in legal language, means not the property itself, but the kind of interest which a person has in certain real property, whether the absolute ownership, a qualified ownership, or only the right to use it for a time.*

2. Estate in Fee.—One is said to have an *estate in fee*, or an *estate in fee-simple*, in certain real property, when he has the unqualified ownership of it; the right to use it forever, and to sell it or transmit it to his heirs. Most of the land in the country is owned in this way. Two or more persons may own the same land together in fee-simple, and in such case are called *joint owners*.

3. Estate for Life.—A person has an *estate for life*, or a *life estate* in certain real property, when he has the right to use it during his own life or the life of some other person. At present life estates are seldom created to depend on the life of any person except the one to whom the life estate is given, who is called the *life tenant*. A widow's right of dower has been mentioned (page 210); this is a life estate.

---

* The term *real estate*, however, means the land itself. Estate is also sometimes used to mean particular real property, or even all the property, belonging to a particular person.

A life tenant cannot sell or mortgage the land, or destroy houses, trees, etc., upon it; neither can his creditors take it. This is therefore a method often used by parents to provide for their spendthrift children. The life estate, i.e. the right to use* the land, may itself be sold or mortgaged the same as other property.

4. Future Estate.—This is a legal term, meaning the interest which a person has in certain land to whom it is to go upon the death of a life tenant, or upon some other contingency. Thus the heirs of the husband have a future estate in land set apart to a widow for her dower. If land is given to A, and on his death to go to B, the interest which B has during A's life is a future estate.

5. Estate for Years.—This is a right to possess and use certain real estate for a definite period of time. The time may be any period—one, a hundred, a thousand years, or even less than a single year. The instrument creating this kind of estate is called a *lease*. Leases and the rights of the parties under them will form the subject of a later chapter (page 242).

6. Trusts.—Sometimes it is desired to grant to one the benefit or income arising from certain property, but not the management or disposal of it, on account of his or her youth, lack of judgment, or other reason. This is done by means of a *trust*, which is a grant of property to one person (called the trustee) to hold for the benefit of another. The powers and duties of the trustee are different in different cases. Sometimes he is merely to distribute property; in other cases he is to control and manage the property, collect the rent or other income, and pay it over to designated

---

* *Use* in this connection includes the right to rent the land to others.

persons; in others, he even has power to sell the land. These powers are governed by the deed or will creating the trust.*

CHAPTER LVII.

DEEDS AND MORTGAGES.

1. A Deed of land is a written instrument by which the ownership of the land is transferred to a purchaser.† A deed is a contract, and we have seen that such contracts must be in writing (page 206).

2. A Mortgage of land is in form a deed, made as security for the payment of a debt, and to become void on its payment. It does not, however, really convey the ownership, and usually the owner keeps possession of the property. It also must be in writing.

3. Contents.—A deed or mortgage of land must, in general, (1) name the person who is to take, (2) describe the property, (3) name the interest that is conveyed,‡ (4) be signed by the person conveying, (5) be sealed, and (6) be delivered. Other things are often included in a deed, but without these it is without effect. The wife of the owner also must sign, or otherwise she will be entitled at his death, if she outlive him, to a life estate in one-third of the property (page 210).

---

* Personal property is often held in trust in the same way. So, also, there may be a life-interest, or future interest, in personal property: but they are not common. It is, however, often rented, like land.

† If it conveys any estate greater than an estate for years it is a deed; otherwise it is a lease (Chap. LVI.).

‡ Whether full ownership, life estate, etc.

4. Delivery.—It is important to remember that delivery to the other party, or to some one in his behalf, is necessary to any deed or mortgage, as it is to every contract. It is the act which gives efficacy to all the rest.

5. Recording.—After delivery the purchaser should have his deed or mortgage recorded in the office of the recorder of the county (or town)* in which the land lies. This is not necessary as to the grantor (the person conveying). An unrecorded deed is good as against his claim, or that of his heirs, to the land. But if the grantor after giving a deed to one should fraudulently give another (or a mortgage) of the same land to a second person, who should have no notice of the first, and who should get his deed or mortgage on record first, the second person would have a prior claim to the land.

6. Acknowledgment.—A recorder or register may not record a conveyance of land without proof that it was executed by the person named in it as the maker or grantor; and if he does, the record is a nullity. This proof consists, usually, in a certificate of a proper officer, on the back or at the end of the deed, stating that the person so named appeared before him and acknowledged that he was the person who had executed the deed. In general, judges of courts and justices of the peace, mayors and aldermen of cities, notaries public, and commissioners of deeds appointed for that special purpose, may take acknowledgments. In New York and some other States the acknowledgment may be dispensed with, and the execution of the deed may be proved by an affidavit of a subscribing witness. Deeds duly acknowledged or proved are, with the acknowledgments or proofs, copied by the recorder, word for word, in books provided for that purpose. But the acknowledgment is not necessary as against the grantor.

---

* See page 52.

7. Covenants.—A purchaser of any kind of property, real or personal, obtains only such title as the seller had. If it turns out to belong to another, that other has a right to it. We have seen that in personal property a seller impliedly warrants that he has good title, and if he has not the purchaser may sue him for the damage (page 219). There is no such implied warranty in real estate. Therefore it is usual for a seller to put in the deed an express warranty to the same effect. There are often other covenants in a deed, such as that there are no taxes, mortgages, or other incumbrances standing against it. These do not give the purchaser any better right to keep the land than a deed without them does, but only a right to call upon the seller for reimbursement.

8. Foreclosure.—This is a proceeding, generally a suit in a court, by which the claim of a person holding a mortgage upon land is enforced. The land either becomes his property or it is sold, and the claims or liens upon it are paid in the order of their priority.

CHAPTER LVIII.

APPURTENANCES.

1. Appurtenances are minor rights, or property, connected with real estate, which pass to the successive owners with the land. Thus a transfer of land carries with it all houses, trees, and everything standing or growing upon it, and all mines and quarries beneath the surface. The transfer of a house carries with it the doors, blinds, keys, etc., although they may be at the time temporarily detached, and not upon the property. Nor is it necessary to name these things in the deed.

2. Rights over Highway.—The owners of land adjoining highways own the land to the centre of the road: the public have only a right of passage while the road is continued. The owners of the soil may maintain a suit against any person who encroaches upon the road, or digs up the soil, or cuts down trees growing on the side of the road. They may carry water in pipes under it, and have every use of it that does not interfere with the rights of the public.

3. Rights over Streams.—Every proprietor of lands through which a stream flows has naturally a right to the use of the water that flows in the stream. Each may use the water while it runs upon his own land, for a mill or other purpose; but he cannot diminish its volume or give it another direction; and he must return it to its ordinary channel when it leaves his land. He cannot, by dams or any obstruction, cause the water injuriously to overflow the land of the neighbor above him, nor so use or apply it as materially to injure his neighbor below him. If a stream flows between the lands of two, each owns the land to the centre of the stream, but they must use the whole stream together as joint owners.*

4. Another kind of appurtenance is where the owner of certain land acquires an additional right over land belonging to another, such as the right of passing over that land for himself and whomever he permits, the right to take water or earth from it, to pasture cattle upon it, to lay pipes through it, etc. Such rights once acquired do not

---

* The rule as to navigable rivers is different. They belong to the State, and the land owners have no rights in them beyond those of other persons.

generally belong to the person acquiring them personally, but as the owner of the land they benefit. When he transfers the land they pass with it to the purchaser without being named. Thus we come to say they are *appurtenant* to the land.

5. Right of Way.—This is the right which the owner of certain land has to pass over the land of another. It may be a right to pass with a team, or only to pass on foot. Without it no person has a right even to step upon another's land or enter his house without his permission. But a right of way is something more than a permission which may be revoked at any time. It is an interest in the land itself, and cannot be revoked. When a highway is out of repair or obstructed by snow, a flood, or in any way, the public has a temporary right of way upon the adjoining land. A right of way must be used for no other purpose than passage.

6. Party Walls.—In cities houses are often built having their side walls in common. The wall stands half upon one lot and half upon the other, and each owner has the right to insert the timbers of his house into it. Neither has the right to take down his half of the wall without the consent of the owner of the other lot. In other words, each lot has the right over the other lot to have the whole wall stand. Without such right an owner can do as he pleases with what stands on his own land. Such walls are called *party walls*.

7. Acquisition of Right.—There are two common ways by which such rights as rights of way, party walls, and other rights which one estate enjoys over another may be acquired, (1) by grant, and (2) by long use. The grant of such a right must be by some written document, as it is a contract for the sale of an interest in land (page 207). But such right may also be obtained by its enjoyment for twenty years

without disturbance, though it was not originally granted.*
Thus if the owners of a piece of land have for twenty years
passed over that belonging to another, claiming a right to
do so, at the end of that time they obtain the right. The
enjoyment is deemed to have been uninterrupted, whether
it has been continued from ancester to heir and from seller
to buyer, or whether the use has been enjoyed during the
entire period by one person.

8. Loss of Right.—As these rights may be obtained by
grant and by use, so they may be lost in two ways: by being
conveyed back to the one from whom they came, and by
not being used for twenty years.

CHAPTER LIX.

LANDLORD AND TENANT.

1. Lease.—The relation of landlord and tenant arises
where one person occupies land owned by another, under
an agreement between them. Usually the tenant is to pay
for its use. It is therefore a contract relation, and subject
to all the rules of contracts (Chap. XLV.). The contract
creating the relation is called a *lease*. A lease if for more
than a year must be in writing and signed, if for only a
year or less it may be oral.† Sealing is not necessary.
Sometimes the tenancy is for no definite period (sec. 9).

---

* This is merely one application of the general rule, that a person who wishes to enforce his rights must begin his suit within a certain period (page 207). In the same way, if a person allows another, who claims to be owner, to occupy his land for twenty years, the true owner loses his land.

† In some States a lease for three years or less may be oral.

2. Rent is a return made by the tenant to the landlord for the use of the land. Usually it is in money, periodically paid, but may be in services, profits, or anything else. The parties may make any agreement as to the amount of rent, and when it shall be due. If there is no agreement as to amount, the tenant must pay what the use of the property is reasonably worth. As to the time of payment, where there is no special agreement to the contrary, rent is due yearly, half-yearly, or quarterly, according to the usage of the country. Where there is no particular usage, the rent is due at the end of the year. If the landlord does anything wrongfully to render any part of the premises useless to the tenant, the latter may leave, and no rent is due.

3. Destruction of Property.—Where there is an express agreement to pay rent, the tenant cannot avoid payment even if the premises are destroyed by fire or flood, even without any fault on his part.* Hence, if land should be leased with a flock of sheep, and the sheep should die, the full rent must be paid. But neither the landlord nor tenant is bound to rebuild houses destroyed by an accidental fire.

4. Eviction is the depriving one of lands of which he is in possession. A landlord has the right to evict his tenant either when the latter fails to pay any portion of the rent due or in any way injures the property. He may also do it for any cause, for which he reserves the right in the lease. But this eviction is a process of law. A suit is brought, and the sheriff puts the landlord in possession. No landlord has a right to take possession of his premises personally, without the tenant's consent.

---

* In some States this rule is changed so as to relieve a tenant from paying rent when the premises are destroyed without his fault, and he surrenders them.

5. Sale of Property.—When property has been rented and is afterward sold or in any way transferred by the landlord to another person, such transaction does not in any way affect the tenant's rights or liabilities. He retains the property, and must pay the rent to the new landlord, who is substituted to all the rights of the original landlord. But if the land should be recovered from the tenant by a person having a better title than that derived from his landlord, he is not liable for rent after his use of the land has ceased.

6. Repairs.—A landlord is under no obligation to his tenant to make repairs to the property, unless he has made a special agreement to that effect. But the tenant must deliver up the premises in as good a condition as that in which they were when he took them, except that he will not be liable for the ordinary wear and tear. He will therefore be obliged to make ordinary repairs, such as the keeping of fences in order, replacing broken doors or windows, etc. But extraordinary repairs, such as the supplying of a new roof or repairs necessitated by an accidental fire, the tenant will not be obliged to make.

7. Crops.—A tenant has of course the right to take all crops reaped during his tenancy. A tenant for a definite time, whose lease expires after the land is sown or planted, and before harvest, is not entitled to the crop; for, knowing that his lease would expire before harvest time, he might have avoided the loss of his labor. But if the lease is for an indefinite time, or depends upon an uncertain event, and is terminated before harvest, the tenant is entitled to the crop.

8. Assignment by Tenant.—A tenant may assign his whole interest to another, unless restrained by agreement not to assign without leave of the landlord. And he may underlet for any less number of years than he himself holds, or any portion of the land that he holds. The difference between an assignment and a sub-lease is that in the former the whole interest is conveyed, in the latter only a portion. They are very different in their effect. In an assignment the person who takes the lease becomes liable for the rent to the landlord, though the original tenant is not thereby released. In a sub-lease the under-tenants are not liable for rent to the landlord, but merely to their landlord, the tenant. The landlord, however, retains all the rights he has against the tenant, and may evict him and all the under-tenants, if the original lease be not complied with. To save themselves from dispossession the under-tenants may pay their rent to the original landlord.

9. Notice to Quit.—This is a notice by the landlord to the tenant to leave the premises. In ordinary tenancies for a definite period, a month, a year, etc., no notice to quit is necessary. If the tenant does not leave at the expiration of the time, the landlord may immediately take legal proceedings to evict him. But where the period is uncertain, as where the tenancy is to continue at the pleasure of the landlord, this notice must be given before eviction can be had. The time of the notice is generally at least as long as a month, and in some cases six months. The purpose is to protect the tenant from being suddenly turned out of his home.

CHAPTER LX.

DISTRIBUTION OF PROPERTY UPON DEATH.

a. Wills.

1. Will.—It is a general rule that a person may dispose of all his property upon his death in any way he wishes, even to disinheriting his own children.* This he does by means of a document called a *will*. The person making it is called the *testator*. If no will is left the property is distributed among certain relatives. In such case the person is said to die *intestate*.

2. Who May Make.—The rule is that every person of full age and sound mind may make a will. An exception is that in some States married women may not. In many of the States personal estate may be willed at an earlier age. If upon the probate of a will (page 77) it is shown that the testator was of unsound mind, or made it under undue influence from any one, it will be declared void.

3. Formalities.—A will must be made in the mode prescribed by the law, or it is void. In the first place, it must, in general, be written.† It must be signed by at least two, in some States three, attending witnesses, in whose presence the testator must sign the will, or acknowledge that he signed it, and declare it to be his last will and testament.

4. Revocation.—A will has no effect until after death. Before death the testator may revoke or alter it in any particular. Revocation may be made in two ways: (1) by burning, tearing, or otherwise purposely destroying it, and (2) by making a new will with the same formalities expressly revoking the prior will. If a will is accidentally destroyed, and there is no intent to revoke it, it still legally exists. If a second will is made and does not expressly revoke the former, both stand as far as they do not contradict each other; but as far as they are antagonistic the later one prevails, as where both dispose of the same property but in different ways. If particular property is disposed of

---

* In some States this is subject to exception, so that children may not be wholly disinherited, or a wife left unprovided for.

† Oral wills can only be made by soldiers in active service, or sailors at sea.

in a will, but is sold by the testator before his death, the will is in that respect void.*

5. A Codicil is an addition or a supplement to a will, and must be executed with the same formalities. It is no revocation of the will, except in the precise degree in which they are inconsistent.

b. Intestacy.

6. Distribution of Property.—The order and proportion in which the relatives of a deceased person, who leaves no will, share in his property, are regulated by the statutes of the several States, which are not uniform. But it is a general rule that all brothers and sisters, when entitled, share alike; i.e. there is no preference of the first-born over the others, nor of the male over the female.†

7. As to Real Estate, if there are children they take it all, or if any are dead their children take their parents' shares. If there are no direct descendants, in some States the father or mother of the intestate will be entitled, in others the brothers and sisters. In some the husband or wife is entitled to a portion whether there are children or not. There is no proceeding before the probate court as to real estate. The person or persons inheriting are entitled to the immediate possession.

8. As to Personal Property the rules of distribution are in general about the same as in case of real estate; though

---

* In some States marriage or the birth of a child will revoke a will, so that the wife or husband or child will not remain unprovided for.

† An *heir* is one entitled to the *real estate* of another who dies intestate. Neither one who receives personal property in that way, nor one who receives any kind of property under a will is properly called an heir.

in some States they differ somewhat. Those entitled do not take possession immediately on death. An administrator is appointed by the court, and he takes possession of it all. After a certain time he distributes it among those entitled (page 78).

SECTION IV.

CRIMINAL LAW

CHAPTER LXI.

CRIMES.

1. A Crime is an offence against the public, the whole body of the people, because it tends to disturb the public peace and to overturn the body of laws which the public has established for the security of life and property of each person. The purpose of the penalty inflicted is not expiation, but simply to protect the community against its future commission. Almost every crime is also the violation of some private right for which the private individual has his remedy (page 80, note); but usually the public penalty is so great that the former is lost sight of, and very often is not enforced.*

2. The Laws of each State define the crimes of which it takes cognizance, and prescribe the punishments. The definitions given in this chapter agree substantially with those of similar crimes in every State in the Union. The punishment for the same crime is not the same in all the States, nor is there in any State an equal measure of punishment inflicted in all cases for the same offence. The laws usually declare the longest and the shortest term of

---

* Ignorance of the law excuses no one. If it did, no law could be enforced.

imprisonment, and the highest and lowest fine for each offence, leaving the exact measure of punishment, except for crimes punishable by death, to the discretion of the judges to be fixed according to the aggravation of the offence.

3. **Capital Punishment** is punishment by death, and the crimes for which it is inflicted are called *capital crimes*. These are now very few, in many States only treason and murder. In a few States capital punishment has been abolished. For other crimes the punishment ranges from imprisonment for life in case of the most heinous crimes, to imprisonment for a few days in case of the slightest misdemeanors.

4. **Treason** is levying war in any State against the people of the State; or adhering to enemies of the State while it is engaged in war with them, and giving them aid and comfort.*

5. **Murder** is the killing of a human being deliberately and maliciously, and with intent to effect death; or killing a person in committing some other crime, though not with a design to effect death. The less aggravated cases of murder are in some States distinguished as murder in the second degree, and punished by imprisonment for a long term, or for life.

6. **Manslaughter** is killing a person either upon a sudden quarrel, or unintentionally while committing some unlawful act not a crime. The difference between murder and manslaughter is in the premeditated malice of the former.†

---

* This is treason against a State. Treason against the United States is another crime (page 176).

† *Homicide* means mankilling in general. When a crime it is either murder or manslaughter. Homicide is lawful when committed (1) by an officer when necessary in the execution of his duty

7. Arson is maliciously burning any dwelling-house, shop, barn, or any other building, the property of another. Arson in the first degree, which is burning an inhabited dwelling *in the night-time,* is in some States punishable with death.

8. Burglary is forcibly breaking into and entering *in the night-time* the dwelling-house of another with intent to commit a crime.

9. Robbery is the taking of personal property from another in his presence and against his will, by violence, or by putting him in fear of immediate injury to his person.

10. Larceny, popularly called *theft* or *stealing,* is the wrongful taking of another's personal property, with the intent to deprive him of it permanently. In some States the stealing of property above a certain amount in value is called *grand larceny,* and is a state-prison offence. If the value of the property stolen is of less amount the offence is called *petit larceny,* and is punished by fine or imprisonment in jail or both.

11. Embezzlement is fraudulently taking with intent to apply to one's own use what is intrusted to him by another. To buy or receive property knowing it to have been embezzled, is to be guilty of the same offence. Embezzlement is usually punishable in the same manner as larceny of the same amount.

12. Forgery consists in falsely making, counterfeiting, or altering any instrument in writing with intent to defraud. The word *counterfeiting* is generally applied to making false coin or paper money, or in passing them; but it is a kind of forgery.

---

to take or prevent the escape of a prisoner, (2) by a private person in self-defence or in preventing any atrocious crime, (3) by any one through unavoidable accident without fault on his part.

13. **Perjury** is willfully swearing or affirming falsely to any material matter, upon an oath legally administered. *Subornation of perjury* is instigating another to swear falsely; it is punishable as perjury.

14. **Bribery** is the offering money or other reward to a public officer to influence his vote or judgment, or its acceptance by the officer for such purpose.

15. **Bigamy** is the crime of having two or more wives, and is also called *polygamy*. These words, in law, are applied also to women having two or more husbands (page 209).

16. **Other Crimes.**—Besides those already named there are many other acts made crimes in most States. The following are some of them: Intentionally *maiming* another by disabling any member or limb; inveigling or *kidnapping; decoying* and taking away *children; exposing children* in the street to abandon them; *opening a grave* and removing a dead body for any unlawful purpose, or purchasing such body knowing it to have been unlawfully disinterred; *aiding* a prisoner to *escape; duelling;** *assault and battery; imprisonment* without authority; *libel; rioting*. There are also numerous smaller misdemeanors and immoralities, such as willful trespasses and injuries to property, drunkenness, gambling, indecent exposure, etc.

17. **Attempts** to commit a crime, though unsuccessful, are also criminal, but the punishment is usually lighter.

18. **Accessories** are those concerned in the commission of crimes though not actually committing them themselves. He who advises, procures, or commands another to commit a felony, is called an *accessory before the fact*, and is punished in the same manner as the principal. One who conceals the offender knowing that an offence has been com-

---

* If either party be killed it is in many States murder.

mitted, or gives him any aid to prevent his being brought to punishment, is an *accessory after the fact,* and also subject to punishment.

19. Arrests may and should be made by any one, though a private person, in whose presence a heinous crime or breach of the peace is committed. When no one witnesses the commission arrest can only be made by an officer provided with a warrant against the offender.

REVIEW QUESTIONS.

Municipal Law.

Civil Rights in General.

1. What is municipal law? Is it regulated by State or Nation?
2. What is common law? Statute law?
3. Name and describe the three fundamental rights of persons.
4. What is slander? Libel? How is each punished?
5. Name the public relative civil rights. How enforced?
6. Describe the duties and rights of a parent toward his child.
7. What is a guardian? His duties and rights? An apprentice?

Contracts.

8. What is a contract? Describe the different kinds.
9. What is the fundamental rule of contracts?
10. What persons need not fulfill their contracts? Why?
11. If an offer is made and accepted by mail, at what moment is the contract complete?
12. What is the considerations of a contract? State the rule as to consideration.
13. In case of fraud or force, may the party upon whom it is practiced enforce the contract? May the other? Why?

14. What contracts must be in writing? Why?
15. How long may one delay to sue?
16. Name the three kinds of remedy for breach of contract.
17. At what age is marriage lawful? What relatives may marry?
18. Is a ceremony of marriage necessary?
19. State the former rule as to the effect of marriage upon the wife's property. The present rule.
20. What is dower? Does it exist now?
21. What is divorce? For what causes granted?
22. What is an agent? Name some classes.
23. State the fundamental rule of agency.
24. When is an agent himself liable to third parties?
25. What is partnership? State its fundamental rule.
26. May a partner sell his interest to any one?
27. State how partnerships may be dissolved.
28. What is a sale? Barter?
29. If goods are sold, but destroyed without fault before delivery, who must bear the loss?
30. When must a contract of sale of goods be written? When not?
31. If property is stolen and sold to one who is ignorant of that fact, to whom does it belong? State the exception.
32. When does a seller of goods warrant the title? When the quality?
33. May one give away all his property? Who may complain?
34. State the effect of non-delivery in a gift. In a sale. In a barter.
35. Define a promissory note. A bill of exchange. A maker. A payee. A drawer. A drawee. An acceptor.
36. Describe acceptance. Indorsement. Blank indorsement.
37. When may a note be indorsed? A bill?
38. What is an accommodation note? May the payee of such a note sue the maker? Who may?
39. Explain negotiability, and its reason.
40. What are days of grace?
41. To whom is an indorser liable? Who are liable to him?
42. What two things are necessary to make an indorser liable?
43. State the rule as to skill and care, in services rendered. In the use of property of another.
44. What is a common carrier? Describe his liability as to goods As to passengers.
45. Name and describe the different kinds of lien.
46. Define the three kinds of insurance.
47. What is abandonment in marine insurance?
48 Who may insure property? Who may insure life?
49. When are ship owners liable for the loss of goods?
50. What is a bill of lading? Describe its use.
51. What is general average? Salvage?
52. What is usury? Its effect?

Real Estate.

53. What is an estate in fee? Estate for life? Future Estate?

54. May a life tenant sell the land? May he mortgage it?
55. What is a deed? A mortgage? May they be oral?
56. State the necessary contents of a deed or mortgage. Is delivery necessary?
57. What is the purpose and effect of recording? Of acknowledgment?
58. What is a covenant of warranty in a deed? Its effect?
59. What are appurtenances? Name some common ones.
60. What is a lease? What leases may be oral?
61. When may a landlord evict his tenant? In what way?
62. What effect has a sale of the property upon a prior lease?
63. Who must repair leased property?
64. State the difference between an assignment of a lease and a sublease. To whom must the new tenants pay rent in each case?
65. When is notice to quit necessary?
66. Who may make wills?
67. May children be disinherited by will?
68. How is a will made? How revoked?
69. Who receives the property of one dying without will? What is an heir?

Criminal Law.

70. What is the object in punishing crime?
71. What are capital crimes?
72. What is treason? Murder? Manslaughter? Arson? Burglary? Robbery? Larceny? Embezzlement? Forgery? Counterfeiting? Perjury? Bribery? Bigamy?
73. What are accessories? How punished?
74. By whom may arrests be made?

DIVISION II.

INTERNATIONAL LAW.

SECTION I.

PEACEFUL RELATIONS OF NATIONS.

CHAPTER LXII.

NATURE AND AUTHORITY OF INTERNATIONAL LAW.

1. Definition of Nation.—A nation—also called a state*—is a body of persons living within a certain territory under a sovereign government organized for the purpose of administering universal justice. Thus a body of pirates, though having an organized government and laws, is not a nation and is not entitled to any of the rights of nations, for its purpose is not justice but plunder. So communities of savages do not come under international law. But there are very few countries appearing on the map which are not now considered entitled to its protection.

2. Sovereignty is the chief attribute of a nation. This

---

* In this connection the two words mean the same. In the United States the latter has a peculiar meaning, for none of our States are nations. Through this division they will be used as synonymous. The rules here stated apply only to the United States as a nation, for the States, as such, can have no relations with foreign nations.

means the full right to govern its subjects without interference or direction from any other power, and the right to enter into relations with other states. All states, no matter how small or how great in territory or power, possess an equal degree of independent sovereignty.

3. Dependence.—There is a sense, however, in which nations are dependent upon each other. Persons in the social state, as we have seen, are dependent upon each other for assistance (page 11). Such is, in a measure, the mutual dependence of nations. Although the people of every nation may have within themselves the means of maintaining their individual and national existence, their prosperity and happiness are greatly promoted by commerce with other nations; consequently there is more or less intercourse between them and their respective citizens.

4. International Law, called also the *law of nations*, is the system of rules regulating this intercourse between nations and their respective subjects, as acknowledged by the Christian states of the world. Like the civil law, it is founded in the principles of natural justice, but is not and cannot be so broad as the law of nature (page 17).* It is made necessary by the fact that nations, as well as individuals, have their rights which other nations must respect, the right of property, of reputation, the right to protect its citizens against injury by foreigners; just as municipal law is necessary to regulate the rights of men (page 12).

5. Of Recent Origin.—As a system the law of nations is of modern growth. It has existed but a few centuries. Nations, even beyond the middle of the Christian Era, were little gov-

---

* It must be remembered that international law not only does not and cannot descend to all the details of justice made obligatory by the divine law, but also that in some cases it allows positive injustice; for it consists not of what most Christian nations *ought* to agree upon, but what they *have*.

erned by the principles of natural justice. Little respect was paid by one to the persons and property of the citizens of another. Robbery on land and sea was not only tolerated, but esteemed honorable; and prisoners of war were either put to death or reduced to slavery. By this rule commerce was destroyed, and perpetual enmity kept up between nations.

6. **Cause of its Growth.**—The law of nations is the recognition of the fact that foreigners have claims upon us. It has always been, and is now to a great extent, a principle of action with all peoples that foreigners are entitled to no consideration. The less that is known of them the less are their rights regarded. Christianity, the spirit of chivalry, and the increasing intercourse of nations with each other, have been the agents which have caused the world to recognize the natural rights of foreigners, and which have built up the law of nations.

7. **Enforcement.**—The strongest distinction between international and civil law is that while the latter has the power of a state to enforce it, with the former there is no means of enforcement, in case of dispute or disobedience. This follows from the sovereignty of each nation. There is no sovereign power above them all. It is and must remain a system of laws which the parties may or may not obey, as long as the world remains composed of separate nations. The only remedy is for the nation injured by its violation to appeal to the sense of justice of the other, generally a futile appeal, or to resort to war.

8. **Arbitration** is a proceeding which has been resorted to at times in the settlement of minor disputes; but there is no power to compel submission to arbitration, or obedience to the decision when made.

9. **Treaties**, as such, form no part of international law. They are binding only on those who make them, while the

law of nations is binding on all nations. But they often contain agreements to do many things enjoined by the law of nations, and if most of the treaties between the powers contain the same stipulations, they thus become evidence of what the law is in those particulars.

10. The Defects of international law are as follows: (1) There is no international legislature to declare what shall be law, and to make changes when necessary; (2) there is no judiciary to apply it in cases of disputes between nations, and each nation must make the decision for itself; (3) there is no supreme power to execute the law (sec. 7), and the injured nation must execute it by war, and if it cannot, must submit. For these reasons the law is uncertain, even at best, acknowledged by but a portion of the world, and very slow to improve. In case of dispute, neither disputant is likely to make a just judgment, and justice is virtually denied to the weak power when against the interest of the strong.

11. Observance.—Having thus the power in their own hands nations do not always observe the law, even when it is clearly established. Even in the latest times it has been flagrantly violated by ambitious princes or misguided people. But comparing its commencement in the Middle Ages with its present position we can say that it has made much progress, and we may hope that in the future, as civilization advances and the principles of justice become better known and more widely admitted, its progress will be still greater.

CHAPTER LXIII.

ORDINARY RULES OF PEACE.

1. Recognition.—Every nation has a right to establish such form of government as it shall see fit, and when established to have its government recognized as such by all others. Otherwise it would be giving one nation the right to interfere in the affairs of another (sec. 6). International law takes governments as they are, without questioning their legitimacy, and thus a usurping monarch is entitled to all its protection. Any other rule would make continual war.

2. Jurisdiction.—The exclusive jurisdiction of a state extends not only over the land within its boundaries, but to all rivers flowing through it, the bays, harbors, etc., upon the coast, and a marine league of the contiguous ocean. The remainder of the ocean is free to all. All nations may use it for transit, fishing, or any other purpose.

3. Intercourse.—International law has not yet advanced so far that intercourse is a right which may be demanded in all cases. In the absence of treaty obligation, or the right accorded by custom, a nation may refuse to allow others to have commercial relations with it, or may prevent immigration into it. It may shut out all mankind. This we believe to be contrary to the true advantage of any state, but the right of sovereignty over its territory implies such a power. But when general intercourse has been once established the deprivation of the privilege, except for some good reason, would be an injury and the violation of a right, for the right is gained by usage. Free intercourse both for travellers and immigrants is now granted by all civilized nations, and it may perhaps be expected that, as the commerce of the world increases and travel becomes more and more general, it will in time become established as a strict right. As to emigration, every citizen now has the right to leave his country whenever he chooses.

4. Travellers while in a country are subject to its laws, and if they violate them, though ignorantly, may be punished by them. On the other hand, they are entitled to the full protection of its laws and its government.

5. Fugitive Criminals.—A criminal must usually be tried in the country where the crime is committed and whose laws are violated. There is, however, no strict obligation upon a nation to return criminals escaping into it. This, too, may in time come to be a principle of international law, for it is now very common to have it provided for in treaties, and our government has *extradition treaties,* as they are called, with several nations.

6. Non-Interference.—It is a general principle that no nation has the right to interfere in the affairs of another, either its internal affairs or its relation with other states. Interference would be a violation of sovereignty. Therefore no nation has the right to aid the colonies, or any portion of another, which are in revolt against their government, while the two nations sustain peaceful relations. Such an act is unfriendly. One may, however, aid another to quell a rebellion, for that is a friendly act. But when the revolt has progressed so far that a new government has been established, and the old government has virtually surrendered the contest, though it may not in words have so declared, the new state, because it is a state, may demand recognition and non-interference from all (sec. 1).

7. Exception.—There is an important exception to this rule of non-intervention. A state in Europe may interfere when the political policy of another, even though it be otherwise just and peaceful, threatens to endanger the security of the former. Thus if one state by uniting peacefully with another will grow so powerful as to threaten the independence of others they may interfere to prevent the union. This is called preserving the *balance of power*, and applies only to the nations of Europe, which have ever been jealous of each other. Extreme cases of outrageous tyranny or cruelty on the part of a government toward its subjects will justify interference.

8. Treaties are Contracts.—As with persons, so with nations, all have the right of making contracts with each other, and when made the parties are under obligation to carry them out. But treaties cannot be made which disregard the rights of others, or which bind to do unlawful acts. So, also, if obtained through force or fraud, they are void.

9. Ambassadors.—These have been before described (page 165). They form an exception to the rule that foreigners always become subject to the laws of the country in which they are. Ambassadors,* their assistants, families and servants, are not subject to the laws of the countries in which they are. They cannot be sued in civil suit nor prosecuted criminally; in other words, their persons and property are inviolate. They are held answerable only to the laws of their own country when they shall return home. The reasons for this rule are, (1) the respect due them as the representatives of a nation, and (2) the necessity that they should be free from all interruption and danger in the discharge of their important duties. They are also entitled to the same privileges in the countries through which they pass in going to or returning from the

---

* We here mean foreign ministers of all kinds.

country to which they are sent. Any disrespect shown to them is disrespect to the nation they represent.

10. **Consuls** are not entitled to the privilege enjoyed by ministers, but are subject to the laws of the country in which they reside. As in the case of ministers, consuls carry a certificate of their appointment, and must be acknowledged as such by the government of the country in which they reside, before they can perform any duties pertaining to their office.

11. **Reprisals** have been before explained (page 147). They are sometimes used as a means of obtaining satisfaction without actual war. The property when taken is kept until all hope of satisfaction is gone, and then it is confiscated.* But now reprisals are seldom resorted to in time of peace.

12. **Embargo** is the detention for a time of all vessels in the ports of a country by its government. When directed against all vessels, national and foreign, for the purpose of protecting them, it is a *civil embargo*. When directed against foreign vessels in time of peace it is called a *hostile embargo*, and is a species of reprisal. Embargo is lawful, but is falling into disuse, except as a measure of war.

---

* To *confiscate* is to adjudge property to be forfeited, and to appropriate it to the use and benefit of the state.

SECTION II.

Relations of Nations in War.

CHAPTER LXIV.

CAUSES AND OBJECTS OF WAR.

1. Rightfulness of War.—A nation itself has rights, the right of sovereignty, independence, property, etc., and is under obligation to protect them, and also to protect the rights of its citizens. The purpose of government is to protect these rights against all the world. But we have seen that when these rights are violated or threatened by a foreign nation or its subjects there is no supreme power to whom to look for redress or protection. Therefore each nation has in itself the two rights of redress and self-defence; that is, it may use force to redress or to prevent the infliction of an injury upon itself or its subjects. War, therefore, though a great evil, is just when used as a means to prevent a greater evil; and war in itself is not wholly an evil, for it has often been the means of bringing back the decaying virtue of a people.

2 Cause.—But war is not lawful unless it has (1) a just cause, and (2) a proper and sufficient object; that is, there must be some cause recognized as just by most nations, and the object to be attained by it must be sufficient to compensate the world for the injury it inflicts. A just cause is the violation of any of the rights of a nation or its subjects. Thus, interference by another with its sovereignty, or independence, seizure of its territory, unjust injury to the liberty, security, or property of its citizens, insults to its flag or its ambassadors, and violations of treaties, are just causes of war by the nation injured against the one injuring.

3. **Object.**—A proper object of a just war may be, (1) to obtain redress for wrong committed, (2) as a punishment to prevent its repetition, and (3) in self-defence to prevent its present commission. Self-defence against unjust attack is always a sufficient object of war. But in many cases the injury committed or threatened is so small as not to justify a war; that is, the object is proper but not sufficient. Injuries to single individuals are often of this nature. And yet sometimes a small injustice to a single person may be done in such a manner as to imply contempt for his nation: in such case the interests of the whole nation compel it to resent the wrong.

4. **Who Judges.**—And yet, as we have seen, the nation intending to resort to war is the only one authorized to decide whether its cause be just and its object proper and sufficient. Others have no right to interfere, even though they should think the war unjust. But if no pretext of right be offered, any or all nations may interfere, for there is no such thing as the right of conquest.

5. **Arbitration.**—It may be said that in justice all peaceful measures to obtain redress ought to be taken before war is resorted to; such as, demand of satisfaction, and offer to arbitrate. This is one of the cases in which international law has not yet reached its highest point, for such preliminaries, though frequently taken, are not necessary to a just war. Indeed in some cases, as of an attack without warning, they are not possible.

6. **Alliance for War.**—By treaty of alliance, nations sometimes agree to assist each other in case of war with a

third power. But when the occasion arises each of the allies must decide for itself whether it will take part, for no treaty can bind one to wage an unjust war.

CHAPTER LXV.

RIGHTS AND DUTIES OF BELLIGERENTS.*

1. Declaration.—When a nation has resolved on making war, it is usual to announce the fact by a public declaration. It was usual, formerly, to communicate a declaration of war to the enemy, but this is not now necessary. Any manifesto or paper from an official source, published in such a way as to give notice to its citizens, the enemy, and neutrals, is sufficient. Every one should be notified whose rights may be affected, so that he may protect them. The recalling of a minister has alone been regarded as a hostile act, and followed by war, without any other declaration, but such cases have not been frequent.

2. Effect upon Intercourse.—The government of a state acts for and in behalf of all its citizens; and its acts are binding upon all. Hence, when war is declared, all intercourse between the two countries at once ceases. All trade between the citizens, directly or indirectly, is strictly forbidden; and all contracts with the enemy made during the war are void.

3. Foreigners within the Country belonging to the hostile nation are, upon the declaration of war, either al-

---

* *Belligerents* are those taking active part in a war; *neutrals* are all others.

lowed to remain during good behavior, even through the war, or else a reasonable time is given them by public proclamation to depart with their property.

4. Private Acts.—Formerly war made every citizen of one state the enemy of every citizen of the other, but now the accepted theory is that it is simply a contest between the governments. Private persons have no right to engage in hostilities without authority from their government. If they do they are liable, if captured by the enemy, to be treated as murderers, robbers, and pirates, rather than as prisoners of war.

5. Combatants are the members of the army and navy actually engaged in prosecuting the war. They may be killed by the enemy. The right to use force implies the right to take the life of those who make resistance. There is little limit to the kinds of weapons that may be used for this purpose, though the use of poison is prohibited. So also stratagems and deceit are allowable, but not so far as to constitute a breach of faith. When an enemy surrenders or is captured the right to kill is gone.

6. Prisoners of War are members of the opposing army or navy captured in war. They may be confined, and even fettered, if there is reason to apprehend that they will rise against their captors or make their escape, but must be treated with humanity. Prisoners of war are detained to prevent their returning to join the enemy, or to obtain from their government a just satisfaction as the price of their liberty, and may be kept till the end of the war. Deserters and spies, when captured, may be shot.

7. Non-Combatants are citizens of the belligerent nations who take no part directly in carrying on the war. Not only are they not subject to capture or any personal molestation, but their property on land is exempt from capture, as long as they take no active part in the war. Marauding and ravaging by an invading army is therefore unlawful.* This follows from the fact that the war is between the governments and not the subjects. But sometimes, when necessary for the support of an army, the inhabitants of an invaded country may be compelled to give up the property wanted at a fair value, or even in rare cases without compensation.

8. Siege.—In the treatment of a fortified town which has resisted and has been taken by the enemy, the law is far below humanity. It is allowable to give the soldiers free license to plunder. The town may also be bombarded, and thus the property and lives of non-combatants destroyed. It is to be hoped that future wars will mark an improvement in this particular.

9. Civil War.—The foregoing rules of war apply not only to war between separate nations, but also to civil war between portions of the same nation, and to war with savages. In the last case it is not justice to treat the savage with inhumanity because he so treats us.

10. At Sea the property rights of non-combatants are essentially different from those upon land. The object of maritime war is to destroy the commerce and navigation of the enemy, with a view of weakening his naval power. To this end, the capture or destruction of private property belonging to subjects of the hostile nation is necessary, and is justified by the law of nations. It may be that in time this rule will be modified, as there seems to be little justice in it.

11. Privateers.—Besides national ships of war, there are armed vessels owned by private citizens, and called *priva-*

---

* Even the public property of a nation may not be captured or destroyed by the enemy, unless used for war purposes; but forts and other military buildings and stores may be.

International law does not allow the interest of a hostile nation or its subjects in the public funds of its enemy to be confiscated.

teers. Their owners receive from the government a commission to go on the seas, and to capture any vessel of the enemy and its cargo, whether it is owned by the government or by private citizens, and whether it is armed or not. And to encourage privateering the government allows the owner and crew of a privateer to keep the property captured as their own (page 148). But privateering is little more than legalized piracy. Many nations have agreed to give it up.

12. Prize is property captured from an enemy at sea. In reality it belongs to the government, but is distributed as a reward among the captors. Whether captured by a national vessel or a privateer it must first be brought into a port, where a court examines into the facts, and distributes it to those entitled.

13. Truce.—This is an agreement to suspend hostilities temporarily. It may be for a few days, or for years, and for any purpose. A truce binds the contracting parties from the time it is made; but individuals of the nation are not responsible for its violation before they have had due notice of it. For all prizes taken after the time of its commencement the government is bound to make restitution. During the cessation of hostilities each party may, within his own territories, continue his preparations for war without being charged with a breach of good faith.

14. Treaty of Peace.—War is generally terminated, and peace secured, by *treaties of peace*. They leave the contracting parties no right to take up arms for the same cause. The parties to a treaty of peace are bound by it from the time it is made, and a government is bound to order and enforce the restitution of property captured subsequently to the conclusion of the treaty. But, as in the case of a truce, persons are not held responsible for any hostile acts committed before the treaty was known,

CHAPTER LXVI.

RIGHTS AND DUTIES OF NEUTRALS.

1. Neutral Territory.—A neutral nation may insist that neither belligerent shall carry on operations against the enemy upon its territory. It may even forbid the transportation of troops across it. No captures can be made within its jurisdiction on land or sea.

2. Neutrality.—A neutral nation is bound to observe a strict impartiality toward the parties at war. If it aids one party it may be treated as an enemy by the other. A loan of money to one of the belligerents, allowing the enlistment of troops or equipment of war-vessels within the neutral territory, or supplying it with other means of carrying on a war, if done with the view of aiding it in the war, would be a violation of neutrality.

3. Aid by Subjects.—But a neutral nation is not required to keep its subjects within such strict lines of neutrality as it is itself bound by. Private persons belonging to the neutral nation may lend money to either belligerent by buying its bonds, or may enlist in its armies, without involving their own nation. Such things are difficult to prevent. But it is a violation of neutrality for a neutral nation to allow its subjects to equip private vessels for privateers and accept letters of marque in the interest of one of the belligerents.

4. Trade.—In general, the rule is that a neutral nation may continue its customary trade with either belligerent during the war, although such trade may furnish it the means of carrying on the war.* Hence goods belonging

---

*This is the rule. The cases of contraband goods (sec. 5) and blockade (sec. 7) are exceptions to it.

to neutrals cannot be captured by either belligerent, even though they are in vessels belonging to subjects of one of the belligerent powers, though in such case the vessel may be captured; and the goods belonging to the subjects of one belligerent nation may not be captured by the other when found in neutral vessels. In other words, the only property which may be captured by a belligerent is property belonging to the other belligerent or its subjects, when found at sea in vessels belonging to the latter nation or its subjects, and outside the jurisdiction of any neutral state.

5. **Contraband of War.**—But there are certain articles (called *contraband of war*) which neutrals have no right to supply to either belligerent, because they are directly useful in the prosecution of the war. What these articles are, it is impossible to say with precision, as some may in certain cases be lawfully carried, which would be justly prohibited under other circumstances. The matter is very often regulated by treaty. Among the articles usually contraband are arms, cannon, ammunition, ships, horses, and sometimes materials for ship-building, naval stores, or even provisions. Contraband goods intended for one belligerent may be seized and confiscated by the other, no matter to whom they belong, when captured outside of neutral territory.

6. **Right of Search.**—To prevent the conveyance of contraband goods the law of nations gives a belligerent nation the *right of search;* that is, the right, in time of war, to search neutral vessels to ascertain their character and what articles are on board. A neutral vessel refusing to be searched by a lawful cruiser would thereby render herself liable to condemnation as a prize. Private merchant vessels only are subject to search; the right does not extend to neutral public ships of war.

7. **Blockade.**—One of the rights of a belligerent nation

which a neutral is bound to regard is the right of blockade. A war blockade is the closing of an enemy's ports, to prevent all vessels from coming out or going in. The object of a blockade is to hinder supplies of arms, ammunition, and provisions from entering, with a view to compel a surrender by hunger and want, without an attack. A neutral vessel attempting to enter or depart may be seized and confiscated. Towns and fortresses also may be shut up by posting troops at the avenues.

8. **Paper Blockade.**—A simple decree or order declaring a certain coast or country in a state of blockade does not constitute a blockade. A force must be stationed there competent to maintain the blockade, and to make it dangerous to enter. Without such a force it is called a *paper blockade*. And it is necessary that the neutral should have due notice of the blockade, to subject his property to condemnation and forfeiture. According to modern usage, if a place is blockaded by sea only trade with it by a neutral nation may be carried on by inland communication. And a neutral vessel, loaded before the blockade was established, has a right to leave the port with her cargo.

REVIEW QUESTIONS.

INTERNATIONAL LAW.

Peaceful Relations of Nations.

1. What is a nation? Is New York State a nation? Why?
2. What is sovereignty?
3. Define international law. How old is it?
4. Name the chief causes of its growth.
5. How is it enforced? Why?
6. Are treaties a part of international law?
7. Name its defects, and why they are such.
8. What is the right of recognition? Do usurpers have it?
9. State the jurisdiction of a nation.
10. How far is commercial intercourse between nations a right? May a state prevent immigration? May it prevent emigration?
11. To what laws are foreigners travelling in a country subject? State the exception to that rule, and its two reasons.
12. What is extradition? Is it demandable as a right?
13. State the rule of non-intervention. What is the balance of power?
14. May provinces in revolt be aided by a foreign nation? Why? May a nation be aided in a war with its provinces?
15. What are reprisals? Embargo? Their object?

Relations of Nations in War.

16. What are belligerents? Neutrals?
17. Why is war right? What two general rights does it rest upon?
18. What three things are necessary to a just war?
19. Name some just causes of war.

20. Name the proper objects of war.
21. May a neutral nation prevent a war because it is unjust?
22. Is there any obligation to arbitrate?
23. To whom should notice of a state of war be given? Why?
24. What is the effect of war upon trade between the belligerents? Between a belligerent and neutral? Between neutrals?
25. What is the effect of war upon foreigners within the hostile nation?
26. May private individuals take part in the war?
27. Who may be put to death in war? What means may be used? What deceit?
28. May prisoners of war be put to death? Deserters? Spies?
29. What are non-combatants? May they be made prisoners? Is their property subject to capture, on land? At sea?
30. What are privateers? Prize?
31. What is a truce? A treaty of peace? From what time do they bind individuals?
32. What rights have nations at war over neutral territory?
33. State the rule of neutrality.
34. What aid may neutral subjects render?
35. State the rule as to neutral trade. Its two exceptions.
36. What property may be captured in war?
37. Define contraband of war. What articles are contraband?
38. What is the right of search?
39. What is the right of blockade? The penalty? What is a paper blockade?

INDEX.

	PAGE
Accessory	252
Acknowledgment (of deed, etc.)	238
Action (at law). *See* Suit.	
Administrator	78, 248
Admiralty	175
Agent. *See* Principal and Agent.	
Alderman	57
Aldermen, Board of	58
Alien	27, 141
Alliance	155, 265
Ambassador,	
appointment	164
exemptions	262
reception	167
Amendment (of Constitution),	
national	181, 183–191
state	25
Answer (in suit at law)	81
Appeal (in suit at law)	83
Appointment. *See* Governor, President.	
Apprentice	200
Appropriation	154
Appurtenance	239–242
Arbitration (between nations)	258, 265
Aristocracy	20
Arms, right to keep	185
Army	72, 148
Arraignment	86
Arrest	84
by whom made	253
Arson	251
Assault and battery	80, 252
Assessment (of taxes)	61
Assessments	64
Assessors	55
Assent (in contract)	204
Assignment (by debtor)	221
Asylum	69
Attainder	153, 156
Attempt (at crime)	252
Attorney	81
Attorney-General,	
national	170
state	48
Auditor. *See* Comptroller.	
Bail	84
excessive	187

	PAGE
Balance of Power	261
Bankruptcy	142
Belligerent	266
Bigamy	209, 252
Bill (legislative)	42
Bill of Attainder. *See* Attainder.	
Bill of Credit	156
Bill of Exchange	222–226
Bill of Lading	233
Bill of Rights	183
Blockade	272
Body Politic	24
Bribery	252
Broker	214
Burglary	251
Cabinet	168
Canal	69
Capital	38
Capital Punishment	250
Captures	148, 269
Census,	
national	125
state	36
Challenge (at election)	29
Charter	57
Chattel	220
Chattel Mortgage	220
Check	223
Child. *See* Parent and Child.	
Citizen,	
defined	140
privileges in different States	178
City	57–60
Civil Law	16
Civil Service	166
Civil War, Rules of	268
Clearance (of vessels)	139, 154
Codicil	247
Coinage,	
by Nation	142
by State	156
Colonies, Government in	91
Colony, defined	90
Combatant (in war)	267
Commerce, regulation of	136
Commission Merchant	213
Committee, Legislative	41
Common Carrier	229

Index.

	PAGE
Common Council	58
Common Law	196
Complaint (in suit at law)	81
Comptroller	48
Confederacy	97
Confederation, The	93–97
Confiscation	263
Congress, Continental	93
Congress (of U. S.),	
adjournment	104, 110
composition	124
journal	103
meetings	132, 167
officers	131
quorum	103
rules	131
Congress, Members of,	
compensation	132
civil officer	104
election	103
privileges	132
Congress, Powers of	119-121, 133-151, 177-181, 188
Consideration (of contract)	204
Constable	55
Constitution, English	26
Constitution, State	23-25
Constitution, U. S.,	
adoption	96
text of	100-124
Consul	165, 263
Contraband of war	271
Contract	202-208
Contract, law impairing obligation of	156
Convention, Constitutional	97
Convention of 1786	96
Copyright	144
Coroner	52
Corporation,	
control by State	70
municipal	50, 59
Corruption of blood	177
Council, Executive	47
Counterfeiting	105, 251
County,	
importance	50
officers	51-53
origin	50
County Commissioners	51-53
Courts,	
national	145, 171-173
jurisdiction	173-176
state	75-79
Covenant (in deed)	239
Creditors, rights of	220
Crimes,	
defined	249
punishable by Congress	145, 177
punishable by the State	249, 253
Crop, right of tenant to	244
Customs	134, 136
Days of Grace	226
Death, distribution of property upon	247

	PAGE
Debt,	
of Nation	190
of State	71
Declaration (in suit at law)	81
Declaration of Independence	93
Deed	237
Defendant	81
Delivery (of property)	217, 220
Democracy	21
Departments of Government	31-33
Departments (national)	168-170
Deposit Fund (of U. S.)	66
Deserter, punishment of	267
Despotism	20
Diplomacy	169
District Attorney	53
District of Columbia	146
Divorce	210
Dower	210, 235
Drunkards, contracts by	204
Duties,	
collection of	139
defined	134
laid by Nation	135, 137, 153
laid by State	154, 157
Education	65-69
Election	28-31
Electors, qualifications of	26-28
Electors, Presidential	161, 162
Embargo	263
Embezzlement	251
Emigration, right of	261
Eminent Domain	70
Entry (of vessels)	139, 154
Envoy	165
Estates	235-237
Eviction (from land)	243
Excise	64, 135
Execution (in suit at law)	83
Executor	78
Ex post facto law	153, 156
Fee-simple	235
Force (in contract)	206
Foreclosure	239
Forgery	227, 251
Franchise	27
Fraud (in contract)	206
Fraudulent transfer	220
Freedom of Speech	16, 185
Freedom of the Press	16, 185
Freeholder	125
Free Trade	138
Fugitive Criminals	179, 261
General Average	233
Gift	220
promise of	205
Government,	
necessity for	13
forms of	19-22
Governor	45, 46
Guardian and Ward	15, 200

Index.   277

	PAGE
Habeas Corpus,	
described	85
suspension of	153
Heir	247
Highway,	
regulation of	55
rights of adjoining owners	240
Homicide	250
Hotel-keeper	228
Husband and Wife. *See* Marriage.	
Idiot, contract by	204
Immigration, right to prevent	260
Impeachment	76, 79, 131
Impost,	
laid by Nation	134, 135
laid by State	64
Indians, commerce with	140
Indictment	84
Indorsement	223, 226
Infant	203
Inspectors of Election	29
Insurance	230–232
Insurrection	73, 180
Interest	234
Intestacy	247
Joint Owner	235
Judge,	
of national court	165
of state court	79
Judgment	83
Jurisdiction, kinds of	76
Jury,	
grand jury	84
trial by	81
protected	186, 187
Justice of the Peace	77
Landlord and Tenant	242–245
Larceny	251
Laws,	
defined	12
classified	16, 17, 196
making of	
in Nation	132, 133
in State	40–44
Lease	236, 242–245
Legal Tender	156
Legislature, of Nation. *See* Congress.	
Legislature, of State,	
how constituted	34–37
meetings and organization	37–40
Letters of Marque	147, 155
Libel	198
Liberty	15
Lien, kinds of	213, 218, 219, 232
Lieutenant-Governor	33, 47
Lunatic, contract by	204
Majority (in election)	31
Manslaughter	250
Marque. *See* Letters of Marque.	

	PAGE
Marriage	208–211
Master and Servant	15, 201
Master (of vessel), authority of	233
Mayor	57
Measures, standard of	143
Message,	
of Governor	40
of President	167
Militia	72–74, 149
Minister. *See* Ambassador.	
Minor. *See* Infant.	
Monarchy	19
Money, what is	143
See Coinage.	
Mortgage	220, 237
Murder	250
Nation, character of	90, 97, 256
National Guard	74
Naturalization	141
Navigation, regulation of	137, 139
Navy	148
Negotiable Paper	219, 225
Negro, rights of	28, 189, 190
Neutrals,	
who are	266
rights and duties of	270–272
New States	179
Non-combatants (in war),	
on land	267
at sea	268
Note, promissory	221–228
Notice to Quit	245
Oath of office	182
Ordinance (of city)	58
Overseers of the Poor	55
Paper Blockade	272
Pardon	46, 164
Parent and Child	15, 199, 200
Partnership	214–217
Party Wall	241
Patent	144, 169
Patriarchal Government	19
Pauper	28, 55
Pension	160
Perjury	252
Personal Property	61
Petition (legislative)	41
Petition, right of	185
Piracy	145
Plaintiff (in suit at law)	80
Plea (in suit at law)	81
Pleading (in suit at law)	81
Plurality (in election)	30
Policy (of insurance)	231
Poll	29, 60
Polygamy. *See* Bigamy.	
Poor. *See* Pauper.	
Postmaster-General	170
Post-office	143
Preamble (of U. S. Constitution)	124
Premium (in insurance)	230

	PAGE
President (of U. S.),	
election	161, 188
powers and duties	163-168
qualifications	163
salary	164
term of office	130
Principal and Agent	211-214
Prison	71
Prisoner of War	267
Privateer	148, 268
Prize	269
Probate (of will)	77
Prohibitions,	
on the States	155-159
on the United States	152-155
Property, basis of right of	12
Prosecuting Attorney	53
Protection	138
Quarantine	140
Quorum,	
in National Legislature	103
in State Legislature	39
Railroad	70
Real Estate, defined	61, 235
Rebellion,	
defined	73
aid by foreign nation	261
Record (of deed, etc.)	238
Records, of one State in another	178
Recorder	52
Register	52
Registration (of voters)	30
Registry (of vessels)	189
Release, from debts	221
Religion, freedom of	184
Rent	243
Repairs (to rented property)	244
Representatives, House of,	
national	124-128, 189
state	35, 36
Reprieve	46, 164
Reprisal	148, 263
Republic	21, 23
Revenue Bills	133
Revolution, Causes of the	91-93
Rights,	
defined	13
how forfeited	14
classified	14-18
Road. See Highway.	
Robbery	251
Sale	217-220
Salvage	233
Schools, Common	65-69
Schools, Normal	68
School Funds	66
Search, right of (in war)	271
Search-warrant	186
Seat of Government	38, 146

	PAGE
Secretary	
of State	48, 168
of the Treasury	169
of the Interior	169
of War	169
of the Navy	169
Seizure	186
Selectmen (of town)	54
Senate,	
national	124, 128-131
state	34-37
Sergeant-at-arms	39
Servant. See Master and Servant.	
Services	205, 228-230
Sheriff	52
Shipping, law of	232-234
Siege	268
Slander	197
Slaves,	
apportionment of Representatives	126, 127
fugitive	179
Slavery, abolition of	189
Slave-Trade	152
Soldiers, in private houses	185
Sovereignty	256
Speaker	38, 131
Spy, punishment of	267
State.	
admission of	179
suit against	188
not a nation	256
Statement (by civil officers)	154
State's Attorney	53
Statute	196
Stock, State	71
Stratagem (in war)	267
Stream, rights of adjoining owner	240
Sub-lease	245
Subpœna	82
Suit, proceedings in,	
civil	80-84
criminal	84-87
Suffrage	26
Summons (in suit at law)	80
Supervisors	54
Supervisors, Board of	51
Tariff	135
Tax.	
by Nation	134-136, 153
by State	60-65, 157
Tenant. See Landlord and Tenant.	
Tender. See Legal Tender.	
Territories,	
how governed	21, 180
represented in Congress	128
Test Oath	182
Theocracy	19
Title of Nobility	154, 157
Tonnage	158
Town Officers	54-56
Town Meeting	56
Township	54

	PAGE
Treason,	
against Nation	176, 177
against State	250
Treasurer,	
state	48
county	51
town	55
Treaty,	
defined	164
by whom made	164
State forbidden to make	155
as part of international law	258, 262
Treaty of Peace	269
Trial	82, 85
See also Jury.	
Truce	269
Trust	236
Usury	234
Vacancy,	
in State Legislature	37
in Congress	102
Verdict	82
Vessels. *See* Entry, Clearance, Registry, Shipping.	

	PAGE
Veto,	
by Governor	43, 44
by President	133
Voters. *See* Electors.	
Village	58–60
War,	
power of Congress over	147–150
by States	158
by private persons	267
rightfulness of	264
just causes of	264
objects of	265
effect upon belligerents	266
effect upon neutrals	270
Ward. *See* Guardian and Ward.	
Warranty,	
of title	219, 239
of quality	219
Way, Right of	241
Weights, standard of	143
Wife,	
power to contract	204
property rights	209
right of support	210
See Marriage.	
Will	78, 245–248

www.ingramcontent.com/pod-product-compliance
Lightning Source LLC
LaVergne TN
LVHW050914030125
800405LV00041B/1155